NELSON ALGREN

NELSON ALGREN

A Collection of Critical Essays

Edited by
Robert Ward

Madison • Teaneck
Fairleigh Dickinson University Press

Associated University Presses
2010 Eastpark Boulevard
Cranbury, NJ 08512

The paper used in this publication meets the requirements of the American National Standard for Permanence of Paper for Printed Library Materials Z39.48–1984.

Library of Congress Cataloging-in-Publication Data

Nelson Algren : a collection of critical essays / edited by Robert Ward.
p. cm.
Includes index.
ISBN-10: 0-8386-4108-3 (alk. paper)
ISBN-13: 978-0-8386-4108-8 (alk. paper)
1. Algren, Nelson, 1909-1981—Criticism and interpretation. I. Ward, Robert, 1966-

PS3501.L4625Z78 2007
813'.52—dc22

2006016569

PRINTED IN THE UNITED STATES OF AMERICA

For the novelist's place has traditionally been on the side of the loser. I can see no purpose in writing about people who seem to have won everything.

Nelson Algren

Contents

Acknowledgments

THE MAJORITY OF THE ESSAYS COLLECTED IN THIS VOLUME WERE delivered at Nelson Algren: An International Symposium, which took place at the University of Leeds in the summer of 2000. The transition between that event and this volume of essays has been a lengthy one and I should like to thank all the contributors for their enduring patience and enthusiasm.

I should also like to thank the following people for their encouragement and support: Mick Gidley, Alistair Stead, T. J. Dowling and the American Embassy in London, Paula Plainter, Art Shay, Steve Longstaffe, Jason Lee, Bill Savage, and Carlo Rotella. Also, to close friends: Caroline Sumpter, Richard Haw, John Braime, Jason Mulloy, Nick Bandu, Dan O'Connor, Warren Leming, Sean Davidson, Colin Winborn, and, my wife, Suzannah Camm.

Introduction

NELSON ALGREN IS ONE OF THE MOST IMPORTANT, YET CRITICALLY undervalued, American writers to have emerged from the literary and intellectual milieu of the 1930s. After *Somebody in Boots* (1935)—a novel shaped by his personal experience of the economic and social turmoil of the Depression—the years from 1942 to 1956 represented the finest period of his work. *Never Come Morning* (1942), *The Neon Wilderness* (1947), *The Man with the Golden Arm* (1949), *Chicago: City on the Make* (1951), and *A Walk on the Wild Side* (1956) are the books that established his reputation as a writer preoccupied with the underside of urban life. The numerous portraits of addicts and dealers, prostitutes, pimps, tricksters, and petty hustlers are shaped by a vision that is both harshly realistic and intensely poetic, capturing what one reviewer calls "the terrible beauty of hopeless lives."[1]

Of the achievements that highlight Algren's place in the history of American letters, perhaps none is more significant than the reception given *The Man with the Golden Arm*. That novel, which highlighted contemporary issues of narcotic addiction and institutional corruption pervading American society after World War II to frame the tragic character Frankie Machine, won in 1950 the first National Book Award for fiction. Like *Never Come Morning*, the novel was a best-seller and was adapted for cinema, though somewhat controversially, by Otto Preminger in 1955.[2] Despite such critical and commercial success, Algren's position as one of the seminal writers of midcentury America was not to last.

In a series of interviews conducted by H. E. F. Donohue in 1962 and 1963, Algren showed dismay at his diminishing status—his work overlooked or treated disparagingly while that of other contemporary novelists was accorded critical attention. Particular reviews—Leslie A. Fiedler's "The Noble Savages of Skid Row," for instance, which used *A Walk on the Wild Side* to slate Algren as "almost a museum piece . . . whose fictional world is at the ultimate remove from any reality his readers know"—must have contributed to that anxiety.[3] And Algren, who wrote "autobiographically—I mean emotionally, you know," became increasingly vulnerablc and cmbittered by such attacks.[4]

Apart from a few influential articles, most notably George Bluestone's "Nelson Algren" in 1957, no substantial study of Algren's work existed until Martha Heasley Cox and Wayne Chatterton wrote the first critical biography in 1975. After his death in 1981, renewed interest in Algren brought about the publication of three major studies: James R. Giles's *Confronting the Horror: The Novels of Nelson Algren*, Bettina Drew's biography *Nelson Algren: A Life on the Wild Side*, both published in 1989, and Carla Cappetti's *Writing Chicago: Modernism, Ethnography and the Novel*, published in 1993. Those definitive works helped stimulate the dynamic breadth of scholarship on Algren's corpus that was to follow in the succeeding years.

This collection, which is the first critical reader devoted to the writings of Algren, includes essays by many of those scholars. Nearly all of the contributions were delivered as papers at Nelson Algren: An International Symposium, which took place at the University of Leeds in June 2000. The reprinting of all of Algren's major work—together with publication of *The Texas Stories of Nelson Algren* (1995), Simone de Beauvoir's *A Transatlantic Love Affair* (1998), Carlo Rotella's *October Cities: The Redevelopment of Urban Literature* in 1998, and *The Man with the Golden Arm: 50th Anniversary Critical Edition* (1999)—reflects the renewed critical interest that surrounded and invigorated that event.

The sequence of the essays in this volume roughly reflects the chronological order of the books or the particular surveys of critical and historical debate to which they refer. The keynote address at the symposium—Bettina Drew's "Nelson Algren: An American Outsider"—opens this collection with a discussion of certain cultural and literary influences. According to Drew, those influences appear more European than American, owing much to the nineteenth-century naturalism of writers such as Alexander Kuprin and Fyodor Dostoyevsky and their critiques of contemporary ideology.

In cold war America, though, such attention was invariably associated with communist discourse left over from the proletarian literary scene some twenty years earlier, of which Algren was a key figure. Drew goes on to note that in such an atmosphere of political paranoia and censorship as marked the 1950s, Algren's life was exposed to scrutiny, and, perhaps consequently, his work became displaced from the formation of a midcentury canon. Thus, in an interview with the *New Orleans Review* in 1969, we read Algren's reflecting back on and questioning his own worth as a writer "not just because the world is falling apart, but that my own seams aren't as tight as they were twenty years ago."[5]

With such anxiety, Algren rewrote *Somebody in Boots* as *A Walk on the Wild Side*—the last novel published in his lifetime. The strategy of recycling stock items to fit different times and experiences was a feature of Algren's aesthetic that allowed him to make clear the transhistorical link between human destitution and social injustice. In such terms, we can better evaluate the reasons for the new prefaces that appeared in the republication of *Never Come Morning* in 1962 and of *Somebody in Boots* three years later.

In "Nelson Algren's Self-Portrait as Meaningful Structure," Frédéric Dumas concerns himself with the second of those prefaces with reference to later short story collections and travel narratives such as *Who Lost an American?* (1963), *Notes from a Sea Diary: Hemingway All the Way* (1965), and *The Last Carousel* (1973). Drawing on the theories of Michel Beaujour, the essay investigates how this corpus represents a series of autobiographical fragments within which Algren searches for personal and authorial identities.

Three contributors offer rereadings of *Never Come Morning.* This was the first of Algren's novels to deal exclusively with Chicago and an area known as the Polish Triangle, which had gained a reputation as "an old time proving ground for Chicago hoodlums."[6] Stephen Hardman sees the depiction of that environment as crossing into the spectacles or urban experiences theorized by Walter Benjamin. "A World of Ruins: Nelson Algren and Walter Benjamin's Destructive Character" teases out the stance against political conformity that both writers shared and articulated in their work. "Spatial Enclosures in Nelson Algren's *Never Come Morning*" is the title of my essay, which especially covers the intersections the text makes between urban and institution-al landscapes. My thesis is that those spaces are perpetually invigorated by the dynamic ambitions of the character. But the conflict between dreams and their almost inevitable defeat patterns throughout the book, a conflict that is for Algren, as it was for F. Scott Fitzgerald, unsettlingly American.

In the third piece to address that particular book, Kasia Boddy examines the tension between Algren's need for journalistic detachment from certain aspects of his subject and his search for an enduring connection with it. In "Detachment, Compassion, and Irritability: The Naturalism of *Never Come Morning*," Boddy examines that tension further with reference to such key naturalist texts as Stephen Crane's *Maggie: A Girl of the Streets* (1893) and Richard Wright's *Native Son* (1940) and their influence on Algren's authorial concerns.

James R. Giles's "Making Nakedness Visible: Narrative Perspective in Nelson Algren's *The Man with the Golden Arm*" continues the interrogation of naturalism. The essay treats literary naturalism as having maintained a distance between the middle-class reader and the world of poverty and delinquency inhabited by the character. But, as Giles suggests, *The Man with the Golden Arm* reduces or, better, "undercuts" such distance, forcing the reader to confront a shared human condition of vulnerability and absurdity. The reluctance to view those characters as grotesque is echoed in "Textual Outlaws: The Colonized Underclass in Nelson Algren's *The Man with the Golden Arm*." Rather, as Ian Peddie contends, the book deserves a reading that engages with a postcolonial discourse of "difference" and "Otherness." Using such a critical frame reveals the ideological relationship that ultimately damages both colonizer and colonized.

Caroline Gottschalk-Druschke's essay, "The City That Turned the White Sox Black: Post–World War II Chicago Boosterism and the Negation of Nelson Algren," looks at the prose poem *Chicago: City on the Make*. In Druschke's view, the text's image of the city as one of desperate poverty and labor struggle, institutional corruption, and violence conflicted with the official and more conservative version that promoted Chicago as an economically and democratically vibrant urban center. Because that tension was articulated during the cold war atmosphere of the 1950s, the text was received as "outdated" and even "dangerous," a reception that, says Druschke, influenced the critical assault on Algren's work during that period.

In the summer of 1956 Algren received a by-now-rare letter from de Beauvoir. Having finished reading *A Walk on the Wild Side*, de Beauvoir wrote about the central character, Dove Linkhorn: "I don't feel any longer Dove as a living boy, but just a puppet with things happening around him."[7] The inanimate feel of the character was an opinion shared by a number of prominent critics at the time. Alfred Kazin, for instance, complained of the unrecognizable human traits given to the characters.[8] Fiedler agreed, noting that the novel's "people are not rendered as seen."[9] Both critics regarded the characterization as a basic flaw of the book.

Philip McGowan brings Bakhtinian theories of carnival to bear on a rereading of such so-called flaws. The essay "Nelson Algren and Carnival in 1930s America" scrutinizes the physical deformities and sexual perversions investing characterization in *A Walk on the Wild Side*. According to McGowan's probing analysis, which clearly intersects at particular points with discussions of "Otherness" and "the grotesque" pondered by Giles and Peddie, the protagonists represent "staged spectacles of freakishness and monstrosity."

Bill Savage's "'It Was Dope!': The Paperback Revolution and the Literary Reputation of Nelson Algren" claims that "devaluation" of Algren's literary output was in part shaped by its marketing and packaging. The essay illustrates the extent to which sensationalist cover designs and blurbs, associated with "pulp" and therefore "inferior" literature, framed the reception and, ultimately, the absence of Algren's most accomplished work from the American literary canon.

Finally, the collection is supplemented by two pieces that serve to enhance our understanding of the personal and public worlds of Algren. In "Hanging with Nelson Algren: A Brief Look at the Author and His Milieu," Warren Leming tells of his friendship with the author, and he maps the radical political and intellectual history that Algren documents in his writings. According to Leming, this places Algren as one of the seminal writers of Chicago's left-wing literary tradition leading up to and beyond the 1930s. Second, as the title of the essay—"The Nelson Algren Archive at the

Ohio State University Libraries"—indicates, Elva Griffith details a wealth of unpublished manuscripts, diaries, letters, and photographs that offer an invaluable resource for scholarly research.

A selection of these archived materials appeared in the Chicago Public Library's exhibition *Writing the First Person: Nelson Algren 1909–1981* from February to May 1988. In introducing the exhibition, its curator, Catherine Ingraham, noted that "we are perhaps at the beginning of an Algren renaissance."[10] This edition, as do all of the ongoing works of its contributors, undoubtedly contributes to the development of that critical renaissance. It represents a marker for Algren scholarship, as Matthew J. Bruccoli's *Nelson Algren: A Descriptive Bibliography* did when it appeared in 1985, and as Brooke Horvath's *Understanding Nelson Algren* did in 2005.

Algren's compulsion to "champion the accused,"[11] to "play the wasp"[12] against political dogma and injustice, remained throughout his life, as the 1983 posthumous publication of his last novel, *The Devil's Stocking*, shows.[13] As readers, academics, and intellectuals, we forget such a writer at our peril. Underpinning these essays, then, is an enduring respect for this writer and his prolific, poetic, yet intensely polemical body of work, which is at last being afforded the serious critical attention it deserves.

Notes

1. John Seeyle, "The Night Watchman," *Chicago*, February 1988, 72.

2. For a further discussion of this controversy, there are two principal sources: Bettina Drew, *Nelson Algren: A Life on the Wild Side* (London: Bloomsbury, 1990), see especially 260–71; and H. E. F. Donohue, *Conversations with Nelson Algren* (New York: Hill & Wang, 1964), see especially "The Con within the Con," 101–28.

3. Leslie A. Fiedler, "The Noble Savages of Skid Row," *The Reporter*, January 12, 1956, 43, 44.

4. Nelson Algren, quoted in Martha Heasley Cox and Wayne Chatterton, *Nelson Algren* (Boston: Twayne, 1975), 24.

5. Nelson Algren, quoted in "Nelson Algren Talks with NOR's Editor at Large," *New Orleans Review* 1, no. 2 (1969): 131.

6. Drew, *Nelson Algren*, 126.

7. Simone de Beauvoir, *A Transatlantic Love Affair: Letters to Nelson Algren*, ed. Sylvie Le Bon de Beauvoir, et al. (New York: The New Press, 1998), 524.

8. Alfred Kazin, "Some People Passing By," *New York Times Book Review,* May 20, 1956, 24.

9. Fiedler, "The Noble Savages of Skid Row," 43.

10. Catherine Ingraham, introduction to *Writing the First Person: Nelson Algren 1909–1981* (Chicago: Chicago Public Library Cultural Center, 1988), 5.

11. Nelson Algren, *Nonconformity: Writing on Writing* (New York: Seven Stories Press, 1996), 65.

12. Nelson Algren, quoted in Bob Perlongo, "Interview with Nelson Algren," *Arizona Quarterly* 45 (1989): 104. Algren was responding to Perlongo's question "What is the writer's job?"

13. The novel's central protagonist, Ruby Calhoun, is based loosely on the life of Rubin "Hurricane" Carter, a black middleweight boxer and world-ranking contender from New Jersey. In 1967, after Carter was arrested for the shooting to death of three white people in a Paterson, New Jersey, bar and in spite of the disputable evidence presented against him, an all-white jury sentenced Carter to life imprisonment. By the time Algren began his research into the case in 1974, Carter had already been imprisoned for seven years. Carter's dogged refusal to accept the verdict and his open resistance to the prison system attracted Algren to a story that would reflect his own political and aesthetic stance. For further material on Carter's life, see his autobiography: Rubin "Hurricane" Carter, *The Sixteenth Round: From Number One Contender to Number 45472* (New York: Viking Press, 1974), and James S. Hirsch, *Hurricane: The Miraculous Journey of Rubin Carter* (Boston: Houghton Mifflin, 2000).

NELSON ALGREN

Nelson Algren: An American Outsider

Bettina Drew

OVER THE MANY YEARS I HAVE SPENT WRITING AND THINKING ABOUT Nelson Algren, I have always found, in addition to his poetic lyricism, a density and darkness and preoccupation with philosophical issues that seem fundamentally European rather than American. In many ways, Norman Mailer was right when he called Algren "the grand odd-ball of American letters."[1] There is something accurate in the description, however pejorative its intent or meaning at first glance, for Algren held consistently and without doubt to an artistic vision that, above and beyond its naturalism, was at odds with the mainstream of American literature. And cultural reasons led to the lukewarm American reception of his work in the past several decades.

As James R. Giles notes in his book *Confronting the Horror: The Novels of Nelson Algren*, a school of critical thought citing Ralph Waldo Emerson, Henry David Thoreau, Mark Twain, and Walt Whitman argues that nineteenth-century American literature was dominated by an innocence and an intense faith in individual freedom and human potential. But nineteenth-century American literature was also dominated by an intense focus on the American experience as unique in the world, a legacy, perhaps, of the American Revolution against monarchy in favor of democracy. Slave narratives, Harriet Beecher Stowe's *Uncle Tom's Cabin* (1852), narratives of westward discovery such as Twain's *Roughing It* (1872), the wilderness tales of James Fenimore Cooper, and Thoreau's stay on Walden Pond were stories that could have taken place only in America—an essentially rural and industrially undeveloped America. But after the Civil War, a process of industrialization began that paralleled earlier European movements from landed economies to those centering on industrial and commercial enterprises. The rapid growth of cities and railroads, the rise of corporate business, and the emergence of a mass consumer culture signaled a shift from the old agrarian America most famously articulated in 1893 by the historian Frederick Jackson Turner, who wrote, "[N]ow, four centuries from the discovery of America, at the end of a hundred years of life under the constitution, the frontier has gone, and with its going has closed the first period in American history."[2]

As America shifted from an agrarian nation to one in which urban centers were key, Chicago in particular became the hub of a vast network of railroads and waterways that extracted, processed, and marketed grain, lumber, beef, and other natural resources from the West and carried to those living in the western hinterlands all of the manufactured wonders of the emerging consumer culture. Swift and Armour; Sears, Roebuck; McCormick Reaper; and the other new corporate powerhouses produced their wares by recruiting large numbers of European immigrants to work in Chicago. It has been reported that by 1880, an astonishing 87 percent of Chicagoans were foreign-born or born of immigrants. Two processes occurred with that mass immigration: One was that the cramped and wretched poverty of European cities began to be broadly and visibly recognized in American ones, so that cities began to be seen as evil and unhealthy breeding grounds for corruption and vice. The other, hardly surprising, is that the immigrants took with them revolutionary political ideals that had become current during European industrialization. In the late nineteenth century, America was awash in strikes that sometimes shut down the transcontinental railroad system. The balance of power between labor and capital—a relatively new conflict in America—was still being negotiated and constructed. In Chicago, the so-called Haymarket riot, which occurred in 1886 when a bomb was thrown at a demonstration for the eight-hour workday, was a public relations disaster for those radical and foreign political ideas. So-called perpetrators were hastily tried and convicted, and the word *anarchist,* with its old-world roots, became a code word in an emerging vocabulary of prejudice toward urban immigrants. Governor John Altgeld of Illinois, himself the son of German immigrants, ruined his political career by obeying his conscience and pardoning those still living who had been unjustly convicted in the Haymarket affair. Even at that moment it was still possible, in some way, for government to take the side of labor, but in 1894, when President Grover Cleveland sent in federal troops to crush the Pullman railroad strike, the balance of power was effectively decided in favor of capital.

In the first half of the twentieth century, American writers and other intellectuals, especially those in Chicago itself, attempted to describe the effects of the new world created by unfettered, government-supported capital. And it is not surprising that they embraced the technique of naturalism, which, stressing the importance of natural forces such as heredity and environment, had worked so well for Émile Zola during the European industrialization experience. But the most-noteworthy novels of the American naturalistic movement looked at American life from the inside, just as antebellum writers had: from the point of view of Anglo-Americans coping with the transformation of the American way of life from its rural beginnings. Theodore Dreiser's novels *The Financier* (1912) and *The Titan* (1914) explicated the rise of a common man into a financial tycoon; *An American Tragedy* (1925) explored the unsavory aspects of pursuing the American dream of success and social standing; *Sister Carrie* (1900) exemplified the exodus of Americans from rural and small-town life to the burgeoning cities. Stephen Crane's *Maggie: A Girl of the Streets* (1893) depicted the reduced opportunities for poor American women already there, and in *The Octopus* (1901) Frank Norris depicted the railroads as social and economic forces affecting California ranchers. All of these novels were situated within a context that was noticeably American, and all of the characters had, to some degree, a connection to American land and history.

A notable exception was Upton Sinclair's novel *The Jungle* (1906), an exploration of Chicago's meatpacking industry so entirely from the point of view of immigrant East Europeans that it began in the Old World. The hero, Jurgis Rudkus, and his family are peasants in a Europe where peasants are being marginalized, and they travel to Chicago to find a better life. But the America they find is one most Americans found unrecognizable. It is not a world in the process of becoming, but a world of exploitation completely formed, existing only in the brutish present. Worked beyond human endurance in the packinghouses, always on the verge of starvation, the Rudkuses are further exploited by a real estate industry that sells them a house built on sewage—a house that can be taken back the minute they fall behind in their payments. Upon the death of his family and the fall of his female relatives into prostitution, Jurgis becomes a tramp and in the end converts to socialism. Life in Packingtown has never been better described, and though the plot of *The Jungle* becomes increasingly preposterous, the book caused a tremendous stir. Congressional hearings were held. In a curious comment on American attitudes toward labor in the early twentieth century, however, the hue and cry did not concern the industry's ghastly wage slavery but the filthy practices uncovered in processing meat, and laws were passed to remedy those practices rather than working conditions. The completely European idea of socialism that Sinclair had hoped to inspire in his readers was virtually disregarded.

Algren's first novel, *Somebody in Boots* (1935), which told of life on the road during the Depression, was commissioned by publishers, its subject not entirely of Algren's own choosing. But Algren's first writings on Chicago—college themes that were essentially short stories—focused on the poor: especially East European immigrants and, to a lesser degree, prisoners. As a university student in the late 1920s, Algren had studied more British than American literature and had been deeply moved by the thinking of various European socialists he encountered in sociology courses. His college absorption in literature and sociology was so intense that he made almost no attempt to socialize with his peers, wondering whether it would be worth his while to answer a silly question when he could be memorizing lines from Shakespeare. His earliest literary influences, therefore, were by his own volition outside the sphere of the traditional depictions of the American experience and American identity.

Algren's second novel, *Never Come Morning* (1942), for which he himself chose the immigrant community setting in the slums of Chicago, was in that vein. As did *The Jungle*, it concerned Polish immigrants, and it too depicted the city of Chicago as a completely formed entity whose history and cultural identity were more or less irrelevant to his characters. Indeed, Bruno Bicek and

Steffi Rostenkowski are simply more-recent but direct descendants of Jurgis Rudkus: alienated from the brutal outside world and enclosed in an immigrant world without exit. The only remnant of the Old World in the prostitute Steffi's life is the church, which encourages her to blame herself for her suffering when she seeks solace there. For those characters there is no trace of the American dream of self-betterment; Steffi cannot see past stasis. "'Polish homes,' Steffi remembered. 'Men and women who worked by day in order to sleep together at night. If it wasn't for that they labored, what then was their labor for, she wondered.'"[3] The only connections Bicek and Steffi have to American consumer culture are the images in Hollywood movies and the prizes won at amusement parks. That sense of total exclusion from mainstream American life is significant, and, as in *The Jungle*, it produced a curious effect. It forced the American reader to abandon presuppositions about American life and to "confront the horror," as Giles has put it, directly, as a reader from another country might see it.

Clearly, by the 1940s, Algren's artistic vision was too sophisticated to allow espousing the Marxist political stance that had made *Somebody in Boots* seem so heavy-handed. Under the European influences of Louis-Ferdinand Céline, Alexander Kuprin, and Fyodor Dostoyevsky, among others, Algren aspired to create literature whose themes were central to humanity rather than national identity or ideology, for Algren's was essentially a humanistic vision for all mankind: In his imagination the world was borderless, his Chicago like "the Petersburg of Dostoyevsky."[4] His next book, the story collection *The Neon Wilderness* (1947), included both immigrants and Americans from the lumpenproletariat Algren had experienced during his Depression wanderings, and the lines from David Wolff's poem "The City," which opened the book, suggested one of Algren's most deeply held beliefs: "not walls, nor men / brutal, remote, stunned, querulous, weak or cold / do crimes so massive, but the hideous fact / stands guilty: the usurpation of man over man."[5]

Such usurpation led to Algren's preoccupation with imprisonment, the point in any society at which the individual is face to face with the armed power of the state. He saw incarceration first and foremost from a sociological perspective, as an issue of social control and therefore a mechanism perennially prone to the age-old horror of usurpation. He depicted that in the story "Depend on Aunt Elly," in which a female prisoner gives up her life savings to get parole, only to find herself the victim of a never-ending blackmail, and there is a jail scene in every novel he wrote and in many of his finest stories. He also saw military service as the source of a similar conflict between the individual and a powerful and armed social mechanism, and around 1950 he had plans to write a novel about soldiers absent without leave who had revolted against military authority and set up their own camp composed of outlaws from every army. "It was quite an operation—they had food and guns and trucks and their own women,"[6] as Algren described it. But Algren's essentially sociological and philosophical thinking on incarceration and military service was at odds with a general American attitude toward incarceration as a practical issue and military service as a matter of pride.

While American social organization emphasized individual achievement, Algren had an unwavering belief in collective human responsibility. Algren felt that if we did not know what was happening to the men and women who endured all the tragedies and enjoyed none of the benefits of our society, we then did not know what was happening to ourselves, and he found a life's purpose in showing the American public what was going on in their midst if only they took off their ideological blinders. He hoped, as Sinclair had hoped, that by so doing, he could generate in America compassion as well as guilt and shame that could bring about social change. Algren believed that in undertaking responsibility for oneself and others—a process involving compassion for others—a meaningful life could be created, and guilt, while a heavy burden in Algren's world, is a sign of humanity because it can generate that compassion and collective responsibility. Ernest Hemingway told Algren that in *The Man with the Golden Arm* (1949) he had "beat Dostoyevsky,"[7] and the reference is significant. In the novel's culminating scene, in which the police captain Bednar understands that in failing to have seen that "We are all members of one another"[8] he has condemned himself to a living death, Algren makes numerous references to Bednar's hanging on a cross. Here Algren espoused the importance of collective responsibility through a subtle appeal to Christian tenets acceptable to his audience. And this was a shrewd move, for as any student of American life and culture knows, the idea of collective human responsibility in the United States is a hard sell.

But from 1945 to 1950, as many American troops remained in Europe and as both Europe and the United States were enjoying the victory of a hard-won fight, there was, in America, a brief openness to European ideas and influences. Jean-Paul Sartre and, later, Simone de Beauvoir traveled to the United States to spread their ideas about existentialism, and many European refugees from the war began to build new careers in the United States. European composers such as Erich Korngold were writing Hollywood movie scores, and European architects were constructing buildings in American cities. Scores of émigré intellectuals from Kurt Weill to Bruno Bettelheim were introducing European ideas into the American mainstream. It was during that period that *The Man with the Golden Arm* became a best-seller and won the National Book Award. And later, Algren would describe that brief window from 1946 to 1950 as "very fresh time"[9]—the time in life to which he would most like to return. Though certainly he enjoyed the time because of his personal success, there were also cultural forces at work during those years that made him comfortable and made his ideas more acceptable in his own country.

By the early 1950s, however, that openness had virtually disappeared, and political events in the United States made Algren look at his own country with concern. The Korean "police action," said to be the war to contain communism, signaled to Algren the growing power of the military-industrial complex that Sartre and de Beauvoir feared would start World War III. The House Un-American Activities Committee, the loyalty oaths, and the media saturation with military preparedness prevailed. Algren had long fulfilled what he considered his political obligations by giving talks to civic groups and lending his name to petitions, and now he wrote two long essays on the American scene; the new genre allowed him more room for direct social commentary than his novels. The first was *Chicago: City on the Make* (1951), a wide-ranging and poetic history of the city in which he stated the role of his own work in concrete and politically charged terms: "[L]iterature is made upon any occasion that a challenge is put to the legal apparatus by conscience in touch with humanity."[10] The second essay, finally published only a few years ago under the title *Nonconformity: Writing on Writing* (1996), directly discussed the increasingly repressive intellectual atmosphere in early 1950s America and the rising threat of the military-industrial complex. Stating that "we live in a laboratory of human suffering as vast and terrible as that in which Dickens and Dostoyevsky wrote," he decried Americans' complacency with the new world order and the look of irresponsibility on American faces. "In no other country," he wrote, once again putting America in world perspective, "is such wealth, acquired so purposively, put to such small purpose. . . . Do American faces so often look so lost because they are most tragically trapped between a very real dread of coming alive to something more than existing, and an equal dread of going down to the grave without having done more than merely to be comfortable? If so, then this is truly the American disease."[11]

The language of this essay—existence, purpose, responsibility, dread—was the language of existentialism, the European existentialism of de Beauvoir and Sartre that had found even in Algren's earlier novels an American literary exponent. Algren was a man of European intellectual orientation in an America that was becoming more isolated and more intolerant of outside political thought. His editor, worried, arranged editorial sessions aimed at toning down Algren's message. But in a symptom of the very atmosphere Algren was discussing, his publisher, Doubleday, declined to publish the book because it did not want to be known as a "Red House."

What clearer proof that the stifling cold war cultural atmosphere was everywhere; to try to be a writer in it was to become engulfed; one could drown in it. Algren soon booked passage to Paris; he needed not only Simone but also the international community, who had tolerance and respect for his ideas. But his passport was not renewed. Two years later, in 1955, he did manage to get to Cuba, where American citizens could then travel easily, and was buoyed by its Old World charm and a visit to Hemingway. But having his freedom taken away and being forced to live in a new, powerful, confusing, and stifling political environment damaged him artistically. For six years, from 1953 to 1959, he was an exile stuck in his own land, watching America embrace values that he found empty and meaningless.

Those six years generated tremendous changes in American society. The space race, new science curricula in the schools, and the availability of mass-produced cars, housing, household appliances, and television fueled a technology-driven consumer culture that pushed aside the old railroad networks of manufactured goods and caused the great nineteenth- and early-twentieth-century industrial machine of Chicago to falter. Algren had unwittingly found himself amid a tide of white flight and suburbanization when he personally realized the American dream by buying a house on the Indiana Dunes, and at the end of the decade, he was living in an America that thought it had liberated itself from the cold war by electing as president the dashing John F. Kennedy, the father of young children. The nuclear family was *in*, and it was prosperous; for those who wanted to remain single there was the life of the *Playboy* king Hugh Hefner, who portrayed himself as a pasha 1960s style: by selling sex as a legal commodity and earning respect and millions as a businessman while the girl on the street went to jail and was treated with contempt for trying to make twenty dollars.

In the New World nobody worried about the girl in the street. In the New World everyone was middle class, and everyone was polite: smiling on a man while slapping a subpoena in his hand, defrauding him by contract when he was not watching. The New World excluded Algren, denied him contracts and the right to travel; for lack of money he had to let Otto Preminger's "purchase" of his movie rights go unchallenged. He wrote now:

> To the artist, the landscape of commercial enterprise has always been a chamber of mirages by which the true world is perverted; and the *Milieu-Man*, the critic, has, traditionally, been the artist's apologist.
>
> But to Business, Government, Church, Military, TV, Press, and Hollywood, the world which feeds, clothes, arms and amuses men is the one real world; the artist is the distorter.
>
> The *Milieu-Man*, has now, by and large, become the Establishment's apologist."[12]

The pall of American commercial life seeped into the minds of the middle class and lulled it into happiness with prosperity; the glorification of self-promoted men like Hefner had removed the desire even to find compassion.

The American intellectual surrender to the cold war was devastating to Algren. Derided for writing about, as Otto Preminger described them, "such animals, you know,"[13] he continued to be unable to get a contract for a novel despite his solid-gold literary reputation. Of American indifference to its social woes he said, "I thought I'd make a dent—I didn't make the least dent."[14] The loss in intellectual prestige he had suffered by being censored and financially manipulated by New York and Hollywood was accompanied, for Algren, by a loss in belief that his work was wanted. Algren said that he stopped writing serious novels because of that and because the cost to him was excessive; to continue writing in such an environment, he said, would have been to consider himself an artist with a capital A and not a human being. Of course, when he said that his work was not wanted, he meant in the United States, where responsibility-oriented existentialism did not find a home. Indeed, American writers, as in other cultures with intellectually oppressive regimes, began to embrace a literature of allegory and the absurd exemplified by such writers as Thomas Pynchon and John Barth. After Algren became what he called a "journalist," his work also sometimes took on an absurdist ring, and the titles of his next two books, *Who Lost an American?* (1963) and *Notes from a Sea Diary: Hemingway All the Way* (1965), reflected the alienation from America that he increasingly tried to quell by travel. Later, he would also travel to Vietnam, and the title of the next book, *The Last Carousel* (1973), suggested nothing so much as a sense of loss.

Algren's life and his identity as an American formed an ongoing struggle to insert his ideas into the mainstream of American discourse that ultimately failed. There were works of literature about the disenfranchised, such as John Steinbeck's novel *The Grapes of Wrath* (1939), that became classics, but the Joads were an intact family, as were Sinclair's Rudkuses, while Algren's people are almost always outside such sources of support. Indeed, Algren, who had always been after far larger intellectual game, came to be perceived as being obsessed with "such animals, you know." And quoting F. Scott Fitzgerald, Algren began to wonder how he became "identified with the very objects of my horror and compassion."[15] It happened because in the prosperous cold war years, Algren was associated with the poor, whom Americans no longer found of cultural interest. And indeed, despite the huge increase in the number of homeless people in the past two decades, American writers no longer, by and large, consider the homeless and the lost as appropriate subjects for literature despite the tradition of such work abroad. And so Algren—purveyor of a humanistic and existentialist literature, who once stood at the cusp of literary greatness—found himself driven, under the steam of American postwar culture, down a dark and lonely tunnel into an obscurity that was occasionally pierced by reference to him as a prison writer or a novelist of juvenile delinquency.

Algren's novels and stories, which are now back in print in the United States, generally sell fewer than five hundred copies a year. The exception is *The Man with the Golden Arm,* which sells about twenty-five hundred copies a year and has recently been reissued in a critical edition that sold out its first print run of nine thousand copies. Perhaps Algren's American legacy will be, finally, to be known as the author of *The Man with the Golden Arm,* while European scholars experience him as a rich and complicated writer of intellectual, cultural and artistic significance.

Notes

1. Norman Mailer, quoted in Carla Cappetti, "Urbanism as a Way of Writing: Chicago Urban Sociology and Chicago Urban Literature, 1915–1945" (Ph.D. dissertation, Columbia University, 1989), 9–10.
2. Frederick Jackson Turner, "The Significance of the Frontier in American History," 1–38, reproduced in *The Frontier in American History* (1895; repr., New York: Henry Holt, 1920), 38.
3. Nelson Algren, *Never Come Morning* (New York: Harper & Brothers, 1942), 211.
4. Nelson Algren to Richard Wright, October 22, 1940, Beinecke Library, Yale University.
5. David Wolff, "The City," in *Poetry: A Magazine of Verse* 55 (1940): 169. Quoted in Nelson Algren, *The Neon Wilderness* (1947; repr. New York: Seven Stories Press, 1986), 15.
6. Nelson Algren, quoted in H. E. F. Donohue, *Conversations with Nelson Algren* (New York: Hill & Wang, 1964), 90.
7. Norberto Fuentes, *Hemingway in Cuba* (New York: Lyle Stuart, 1984), 266.
8. Nelson Algren, *The Man with the Golden Arm: 50th Anniversary Critical Edition*, ed. William J. Savage Jr. and Daniel Simon (New York: Seven Stories Press, 1999), 197.

9. Nelson Algren, quoted in Donohue, *Conversations with Nelson Algren,* 330.

10. Nelson Algren, *Chicago: City on the Make* (1951; repr., Chicago: University of Chicago Press, 1983), 81.

11. Nelson Algren, "A Walk on the Wild Side," 46–48. Ohio State University, Rare Books and Manuscripts.

12. Nelson Algren, *Notes from a Sea Diary: Hemingway All the Way* (1965; repr., London: Mayflower-Dell, n.d.), 15.

13. Nelson Algren, quoted in Donohue, *Conversation with Nelson Algren,* 136.

14. Ibid., 94.

15. Ibid., 161.

Nelson Algren's Self-Portrait as Meaningful Structure

Frédéric Dumas

NELSON ALGREN REVISED HIS TEXTS THROUGHOUT HIS CAREER, SO as to include them, more or less altered, in his various books. His body of work is made up of multiple fragments, which echo over almost half a century. The fragmentation can be felt most notably in *Who Lost an American?* (1963), *Notes from a Sea Diary: Hemingway All the Way* (1965), and *The Last Carousel* (1973), which include the presence of a persona who is either anonymous or called "Algren." Many critics have identified this persona with Algren himself.

My thesis is that the question of identity of Algren and the persona "Algren" is the foundation of a self-portrait that gives coherence and that structures all of his writing into a corpus. By creating an alter ego with a problematic identity, Algren gives shape to a metatextual questioning, for, according to Michel Beaujour, "[A] self-portrait is necessarily written by a writer as a writer."[1]

My purpose here is to demonstrate that Algren's search for identity structures his works—to such an extent that it becomes a posteriori a reflection of his creation of himself.

THE CORPUS AS SELF-PORTRAIT

Algren did not write his autobiography; we never find what Philippe Lejeune calls "autobiographic pacts," which are "prologues where the author defines his project and commits himself to the reader."[2] *Who Lost an American?* and *Notes from a Sea Diary* and *The Last Carousel* put readers directly in a universe they are free to apprehend as they wish.

Since the hero-narrator does not have a name, *Who Lost an American?* is not an autobiography, nor even a deceitful one. Were it presented as a novel, either by the author or by the publisher, it could belong to what Lejeune calls a "biographic novel."[3] Yet, *Who Lost an American?* is a hybrid, and neither Algren nor critics have ever termed it a novel. Since it has no formal pact, *Who Lost an American?* is just like its narrator—suspended among several identities—and only the reader is in a position to ascribe it one.

This is why the concept of self-portrait is most relevant: not only in the case of *Who Lost an American?* but also as a key to the interpretation of a corpus that encompasses all of his books. According to Beaujour, "[S]elf-portrait differs from autobiography insofar as it does not have a linear narrative; the narration is subordinated to a *logical* pattern, it pieces together elements, sometimes in a makeshift way."[4]

The corpus of the self-portrait built itself up little by little over the years: usually, many pieces had been published in magazines before they were put together, usually revised. Those fragments of the self echo from book to book, and they use a wide range of effects typical of autobiography and its roots in firsthand experience, which, according to Algren, is the basis of creation.

The Mythical Dimension of Algren's Self-Portrait

The preface to *Somebody in Boots* is the genesis of the entire work; it starts by putting writing at the core of the author's concern:

> I wonder whether there stands yet, above an abandoned filling station a mile this side of the border, a wooden legend once lettered in red—
>
> *Se Habla Espanol*
>
> —that must now have been long washed to rose.
> . . . I'd lettered it myself.[5]

Thus Algren identifies with the protagonist as a writer, although his only creation amounts to only one crude sentence—what is more, in a foreign language. The barbarism in *Espanol* (he should have written *Español*) shows he is incompetent in that language, and therefore his first creation is a blatant lie. Thus, while he is giving an account of the genesis of his works, the author reveals that his writing is closely linked to the manipulation of truth: readers are warned that they are just like the clients of his gas station—that is, targets of a narrative strategy.

We have to note that Algren uses this Texas experience to open "The Last Carousel," but this time the color of the legend is no longer red but green, and the Spanish mistake has gone. This new fragment created on the basis of an autobiographic element is one of the innumerable echoes in his works. The author plays on the presumption of authenticity created by the preface to *Somebody in Boots* to leave readers in a state of uncertainty. He thus implicitly reminds them that personal experience is actually the basis of his writing, but that for him an autobiographic account is only a means to a more ambitious project.

The fact that the author starts his quasi-archaeological search for genesis by recalling a legend almost completely erased, lost in the middle of the desert and of his memory, reveals that he is fulfilling the role of a biblically inspired demiurge. The words, written by a young author in the middle of an urban, postapocalyptic vacuum, are reminiscent of those uttered by the God of Genesis that created the universe, as well as a major literary work. Just as the first volume of the Bible was written after the creation of the universe, the preface to *Somebody in Boots* is an a posteriori writing of primordial events.

In *Somebody in Boots,* as in the Bible, "In the beginning was the Word."[6] The American Adam is called Cass McKay, born in Mexico, in a grotesque environment where death meets exuberance and sterility: "In the small-time vice-village of Matamoros I took a room in a hotel run by a woman who had entitled herself "The Mother of the Americans," though she didn't look like anyone's mother. There I wrote the first chapters of a novel I first called *Native Son*" (SIB, preface, 9). With hindsight, the author is able to assess the meaning of his creation—to such an extent that he inverts its original signification and indirectly begins to identify his hero with the biblical ancestor: "My flash notion of a Final Descendant now appears to be that of a progenitor" (SIB, preface, 9).

Just as all of the other works are, the preface to *Somebody in Boots* is punctuated with echoes, for the narrator structures his account with an obsessive leitmotif concerning the main task he had to perform at that time. Indeed, although he was a gas station attendant, he was actually fooled by his partner into shelling black-eyed peas, hoping wildly he could sell them to the natives.

Just as in *Who Lost an American?* the persona's typewriter affords him the opportunity to escape the company of his fellow travelers, his sign is a shelter in the middle of a hostile environment: "And sat in its shade shelling black-eyed peas below a broken sun" (SIB, preface, 5). This task is his only activity after writing the legend—and before writing his novel. It is thus to be considered as the continuation of the writing process: through the accumulation of concrete, real-life experience.

The analogy between the young man's and the writer's toil is all the more relevant since none of the activities bring in any money. The attendant's gift for writing leads him to sign an impossible contract with the gas company—comparable to the Faustian pact signed by the persona with Doubledge Deadsinch and Pyrhana, his publishing company in *Who Lost an American?* The only encouragement he gets is from his partner, who knows how to exploit the young man's gullibility and his social ambition: "You'll be the Blackeye-Pea King of the Valley" (SIB, preface, 6). Ironically, that prophecy will come true, insofar as the protagonist will actually become a successful writer whose memories will turn out to be his main sources of inspiration. Shelling peas and keeping them methodically in jars are equivalent to gathering memories and keeping them in store for future use: "I was shelling my way to fame" (SIB, preface, 6). Thirty years later, the same process is still going on: "Now I have to go back to my shelling" (SIB, preface, 9). Thus, writing is definitely linked as much to youthful enthusiasm as to chore and to the ungratefulness of the reader.

The Meaningful Structure

The preface to *Somebody in Boots* confirms that when it was published, this first novel fell within the scope of a self-portrait that was being elaborated. The fact that Algren felt compelled to add a preface to a novel he had written thirty years earlier reveals his obsession to have complete control over a text whose metatextual nature brings into play the interpretation of all of his writing and through it, his own identity as an author.

This preface is a fragment that was grafted in 1965. A few years earlier, *Somebody in Boots* had been completely rewritten, and the revision became *A Walk on the Wild Side* (1956). Thus this first novel was treated as a draft, as a manuscript the author had to revise until it reached its ultimate version.

However, *A Walk on the Wild Side* did not replace *Somebody in Boots*; it became yet another fragment in a body of work in which each part is involved in the shaping of a project we may call an interior model—comparable to what Umberto Eco demonstrated about the words of James Joyce's *Finnegans Wake* (1939); "Once the work is completed, each word is a definition of the overall project, for each word concreticizes what the author intends to achieve ultimately: down to its very details, *Finnegans Wake* is a discourse on *Finnegans Wake*."[7] Each book by Algren is composed of units, very often previously published under one form or another and under different titles. Originally, each of them had been devised as an independent unit, and each is indeed capable of reflecting more or less distinctly the author's project. Algren himself says about *A Walk on the Wild Side*: "It's a funny book. . . . It's sort of like an accordion. You can just open it up and play it anywhere."[8] So, although *A Walk on the Wild Side* is a novel, it is made up of fragments, just as *The Neon Wilderness* (1947), *Who Lost an American?*, *Notes from a Sea Diary*, and *The Last Carousel* are. By the same token, by grafting on *Somebody in Boots* a text that falls—among others—within the provinces of autobiography, fiction, poetry, and metatextuality, the author reinforces a posteriori its fragmented structure, whose form and matter reflect those of all of his other books.

In accordance with the subversive principle of self-portrait, Algren blurs the chronology of his autobiographic text throughout his works. This text is scattered among others, or dissolved in them, and readers must make a real effort if they want to make sense of an itinerary apparently devoid of logic.

The multiple revisions of the texts denote an absence of definite authorial strategy as much as a constant reevaluation of that strategy. The self-portrait built itself up as if without the author's realizing it, although he did pay great attention to the sense of his works. Actually, the corpus reflects Algren's technique: "Up to now, I'd just go along with the story and then sort of prop it up . . . plots that don't really stand up."[9]

In his critical assessment of *The Man with the Golden Arm* (1949), George Bluestone justifies Algren's propensity to give a fragmented structure to his novel: "To reject Algren's structure, then, is to reject his central vision."[10] The patchworklike structure can be found in every book and, thanks to the inter/intratextual echoes, becomes characteristic of the corpus. It is what Eco calls a "*meaningful structure.*"[11]

Although Algren kept avoiding a careful planning of his plots (with the exception of *A Walk on the Wild Side*), this does not mean he paid no attention to the structure of his books. As James R. Giles aptly says about *Who Lost an American?*, "The result is a volume controlled by a formless form, a unity paradoxically emerging from Algren's apparent decision to avoid any appearance of unity."[12] Candida Donadio confirms, for example, that Algren "liked to do pieces related to each other so they'd finally be a book."[13]

It is a fact that at the level of the content and mostly at the level of the structure, *Who Lost an American?*, *Notes from a Sea Diary*, and *The Last Carousel* are deliberately disconcerting, and the preface to *Somebody in Boots* actually suggests that such a strategy may also well apply to Algren's "pure" fiction. This preface is fully integrated into the text, because it is congruent with its realistic and poetic tone. Paradoxically, the realistic tradition in which *Somebody in Boots* is rooted is most suitable for expressing such a complex project. Indeed, Patricia Waugh insists that when reading a metafictional novel, we must be able to recognize the type of literature with which we are dealing.[14]

The preface to *Somebody in Boots* is one more attempt by Algren to make sense of himself within the body of his creation; because a self-portrait is essentially metatextual, it enables the author to sublimate his existential questioning by creating texts that themselves express the same kind of questioning. The complexity of the relationships among the innumerable drafts, fragments, or echoes that structure the body of work aptly reflects the complexity of the author's questioning of his own identity.

Far from betraying a weakness in Algren's style, the fragmented structure contributes to endowing his work with a mythic scope. The preface to *Somebody in Boots* leads us to consider the text of the novel—and, by extension, all of the subsequent books—in a biblical perspective.

If the scheme of the self-portrait builds mostly on the question of the problematic identity of Algren's persona, the corpus is not limited to the narratives that involve that persona. As I hope to have shown in my brief analysis of the preface to *Somebody in Boots,* the issue of self-discovery encompasses all of his literary production—to such an extent that it shapes that production into a personal myth. That myth aims to make sense of the author's existence and involves many wanderings, at once physical and metaphorical; that is why, up to a point, Algren's self-portrait can be viewed as Ihab Hassan's "ideal text of quest": "This text will be germane to the forms of myth, romance, adventure, travel, and autobiography. In it, a self, wounded somehow yet acting willfully or whimsically upon its wounds, puts itself at risk."[15] A self-portrait is a fundamentally egotistic project, yet, paradoxically, it draws authors and readers together. Indeed, what readers look for in literature is, above all, themselves, and what they actually discover is an author also looking for himself—in his own texts. In other terms, Algren and his readers find themselves involved in the same quest for identity.

Notes

1. Michel Beaujour, *Miroirs d'encre (rhétorique de l'autoportrait)* (Paris: Seuil, 1980), 15 (my translation).

2. Philippe Lejeune, *Le pacte autobiographique* (1976; repr., Paris: Seuil, 1996), 360 (my translation).

3. Ibid.

4. Beaujour, *Miroirs d'encre,* 8.

5. Nelson Algren, preface to *Somebody in Boots* (1935; repr., London: Flamingo, 1993), 35. Further references are to this edition and are cited parenthetically as SIB, preface.

6. 1 John 1:3 (RSV).

7. Umberto Eco, *L'œuvre ouverte* (1965; repr., Paris: Seuil, 1979), 265 (my translation).

8. Nelson Algren, quoted in John Van der Zee, "The Man with the Golden Pen," Ohio State University, Rare Books and Manuscripts, the Bettina Drew Archive of Nelson Algren.

9. Nelson Algren, quoted in Alston Anderson and Terry Southern, "Nelson Algren," *Paris Review* 11 (Winter 1955): 45.

10. George Bluestone, "Nelson Algren," *Western Review* 22 (1957): 39.

11. Eco, *L'oeuvre ouverte,* 220.

12. James R. Giles, *Confronting the Horror: The Novels of Nelson Algren* (Kent, Ohio: Kent State University Press, 1989), 6.

13. Candida Donadio, interview by Bettina Drew, June 23, 1981, 1, Ohio State University, Rare Books and Manuscripts, the Bettina Drew Archive of Nelson Algren.

14. See Patricia Waugh, *Metafiction: The Theory and Practice of Self-Conscious Fiction* (London: Methuen, 1984).

15. Ihab Hassan, *Selves at Risk* (Madison: University of Wisconsin Press, 1990), 79.

A World of Ruins: Nelson Algren and Walter Benjamin's Destructive Character

Stephen Hardman

NELSON ALGREN WAS NEVER ONE TO TAKE THE EASY ROUTE. HE could be bitter, argumentative, and provocative, yet what unfailingly emerges from the writings on Algren is a sense of appreciation of his idiosyncratic charm. Even his most vociferous critics did not fail implicitly to give Algren his due as a significant writer. Leslie A. Fiedler's scathing review of *A Walk on the Wild Side* (1956) in *The Reporter*, "The Noble Savages of Skid Row," contains phrases of approbation that could very well have been lifted directly out of an Algren novel. The novel's point, according to Fiedler, was "a gin-soaked pill of bitter wisdom," and Algren was "the Last of the Proletarian Writers."[1] Even allowing for the deliberate parody, Algren displayed an unerring and long-lasting influence that was difficult to avoid. When reading Algren, the reader is constantly forced to take a stance, to react in some way; neutrality was not a position Algren took or encouraged.

Critical responses to Algren's work have always exhibited some visceral emotion. Maxwell Geismar in his 1958 collection of essays *American Modern: From Rebellion to Conformity* remarks that "to live completely in Nelson Algren's world is a strange and somewhat exhausting experience. . . . This is a world of ruins—but living ones."[2] To provoke a response was indeed a deliberate strategy of Algren's. His writing aimed squarely at the consciousness of the American public to make visible the conditions of life of those—especially in the urban centers—who he considered were being neglected and ignored. Moreover, Algren's work was a deliberate attempt to make clear the connections between mainstream America and the lower classes.

Algren's tactics were to present in his novels the violence, poverty, and desperation of his characters, but he imbued them with a sense of individualism, compassion, and humanness. Such a project was not without its difficulties, and his concern for his characters, combined with his frequently ambiguous fascination with violence, often led to a negative critical response. Fiedler's review was particularly representative of criticisms of Algren. For Fiedler, Algren was "an exotic" and a "romantic purveyor of escape literature," and ultimately, Algren's sins were both political and aesthetic.[3] Such depictions of Algren as a sentimental and romantic figure with attachment to an outmoded politics deeply affected Algren, who believed that his work was misunderstood, and in part influenced his tendency to isolate himself from the American literary mainstream. Algren has been rescued from that isolation recently, especially in looking past his sometimes lurid and sensationalist stories and toward deeper and subtle methods in his work. The recognition of the influence of existentialism as well as a broader acceptance of the importance and prevalence of naturalist writing in the midtwentieth century opened Algren up to more-sophisticated study. However, Algren's decline, which began in the 1950s, was due partly to his own idiosyncratic behavior. His desire to provoke and his resistance to conformity coalesce around certain ambiguities inherent in Algren and his writing, which, while contributing to the production of his best work, nonetheless contained elements of difficulty that ultimately contributed to his decline. In this essay I examine those incompatibilities and ambiguities in Algren's work through certain affinities Algren shared with the German philosopher and literary critic Walter Benjamin.

I think that a central common concern can be discerned in Benjamin's commitment to read "history against the grain."[4] Put simply, Benjamin's concern over the method of historical scholarship was that it perpetuated a consensus of interpretation that effaced significant portions of historical life and, by extension, distorted contemporary analyses. History was determined by those who were victorious—that is, the bourgeoisie—who presented an ideological vision of the past that legitimized and solidified existing power structures. Benjamin's methodological approaches can be characterized as a commitment to critical practices that uncover and unsettle that false consensus and that reinstate those whom he believed historical practice had neglected. Such critical approaches would then have the effect of reinstating the lower and working classes as legitimate actors in contemporary society. I think a similar impulse can be detected in Algren's approach to writing, for Algren's commitment to the lower classes was based not merely on an enumeration of the ills of certain sections of society but also on the engagement with more-dynamic processes of identity formation. As can Benjamin, Algren can be seen to be disrupting the boundaries of knowledge and assumptions in order to reveal more-fragmented and more-precarious structures of existence.

Such a connection between Algren and Benjamin may on the surface appear somewhat incongruous. Certainly, the Chicago novelist whose preparation for writing was to work out on a punching bag, in his boxing and gambling appears to be a world away from the sensitive, brooding, and physically delicate German intellectual. However, such a connection is not without precedent. Algren's novels were championed by both Ernest Hemingway and Jean-Paul Sartre, and it was Sartre who translated *Never Come Morning* (1942) into French, thereby contributing to its international success. Despite Algren's mocking protests that he had never heard of existentialism, his connection to North European intellectual trends has been well documented and significantly more substantial than his celebrated love affair with Simone de Beauvoir.[5] Algren displayed a deep understanding and appreciation of European intellectual and literary trends, and he was influenced particularly by Alexander Kuprin's novel *Yama* (1909) and Louis-Ferdinand Céline's *Journey to the End of Night* (1932). Those influences are integral to understanding Algren's work in that they supply the necessary link to appreciation of the more complex structures in Algren's novels, which when missed, as evidenced by Fiedler's review, return Algren to a pastiche of 1930s realism. Where a meeting of Algren and Benjamin here is a purely speculative one—and not one with any historical grounding—the two nonetheless appear to share a number of critical concerns and methodological approaches that translate across the Atlantic, including a shared ability to confound and infuriate even their most loyal readers and critics.

My approach begins with a look at Benjamin's "destructive character" in order to draw out some of the ambiguities of Algren's work, especially the way Algren's methodological style merged with his personal attitudes to literature and politics. The idea of ruins, developed out of Benjamin's particular understanding of reversing the notions of destruction and creativity and their connections to urban experience, will be read alongside Algren's *Never Come Morning*. That novel is of particular interest because of the fragmented nature of its narrative structure and the ambiguous depictions of individual agency that may be read by utilizing Benjamin's notions of urban experience. That novel in particular appears to display quite acutely some of the problematic elements that critics identify in Algren's writing: in particular, narrative development and the fusion of politics and aesthetics—two issues that Algren was constantly attempting to address and that caused him innumerable problems later in his career.

Destructive Character

Walter Benjamin's methodological approach was characterized by the personification of ideas, often to actualize the work of the critic. One such individual was the "destructive character," who embodied Benjamin's ambiguous engagement with violence and destruction. For Benjamin, the situation in Germany—where the Social Democrats and German intellectuals failed to counter the rise of fascism—was symptomatic of a disturbing moment in modern culture, and concepts of knowledge and truth were becoming increasingly nebulous. The fragmentary nature of modern experience was for Benjamin easily manipulated by a political culture that presented a homogeneous structure of experience in the pursuit of political power—one whereby the past, present, and future were conceptualized as a natural progression in the name of progress. Benjamin was increasingly disturbed by the power of this linear narrative of history with progress to sustain and legitimize inequality and state violence. Benjamin's "destructive character" embodied a response that would counter that homogeneous narrative with an equal but more ambiguous use of force; truth for Benjamin had, as Terry Eagleton says, "sunk into a deathly sleep from which only a further violation will awaken her."[6] The "destructive character" was a critical response that would unsettle any superficial notions of truth: "The destructive character knows only one watchword: make room; only one activity: clearing away. . . . The destructive character sees nothing permanent. But for this reason he sees ways everywhere. Where others encounter walls or mountains, there, too, he sees a way. But because he sees a way everywhere, he has to clear things from it everywhere. Not always by brute force; sometimes by the most refined. . . . What exists he reduces to rubble, not for the sake of the rubble, but for that way of leading through it."[7] That destruction—or, more accurately, counterdestruction—could take many forms, but central to this was the work of culture. Art for Benjamin offered a means of breaking down ideological formations to expose the intricacies of personal connections and relationships that modern society, with its emphasis on individuality, was increasingly distorting. This so-called positive form of destruction was not a nihilistic one—destruction for the sake of destruction—but one that could allow a rebuilding.

Such a methodology seems to be appropriate to Algren, who was similarly concerned with the conformity that was overwhelming American society. For Algren the violence, poverty, and despair experienced by the lower classes were not conditions that were extrinsic or alien to the mainstream but deeply embedded in the whole of American culture. Algren's response in his writing was twofold: not only to attack the complacency of the middle classes through shock but also to highlight the culpability and responsibility of the middle classes for the ills of society. Furthermore, Algren's own character tended toward an oppositional stance and to continual challenging of any sense of conformity. Reflecting on his early career, Algren spoke of his failure to do that, but his method and his intent are clear: "I thought I'd make a dent—I didn't make the least dent, because there is no way of convincing or even making the slightest impression on the American middle class . . . that there are people who live in horror, that there are people whose lives are nightmares. This is not accepted. The world of the drug addict doesn't exist. The world of the criminal doesn't exist. The world of the murderer doesn't exist. Nothing that does not touch the person individually exists."[8] Algren's approach may be seen as closely related to Benjamin's "destructive character" in that there is an expressed desire to make explicit the destruction wrought by a conformity that continually fails to acknowledge its own culpability. However, such a position is a difficult one to maintain, especially because a commitment to nonconformity can actually reinforce the divisions the writer is attempting to break down. Certainly, Algren's own persona was very much in keeping with Benjamin's "destructive character"—in particular, the fusion of "brute force" with the most "refined" methods of critique, but one that was often self-destructive. Algren's difficulty of seeking legitimacy from the very people he was trying to shock was indicative of the precarious project he was undertaking.

A World of Ruins

An important feature of Benjamin's critique of destruction was the production of rubble or ruins, and it is within the ruins that a radical critique can rebuild. However, as Geismar identified in Algren's novels, the "world of ruins" is an exhausting place. What is important to note is that those ruins have not been produced by the "destructive character" but are merely uncovered; those ruins *are already there.* For Algren the role of the writer was to reverse the conventional notions of destruction and creativity in order to reveal the processes—particularly the erection of physical and cultural boundaries—that had obscured those ruins. A passage from his aptly titled collection of essays *Nonconformity: Writing on Writing* (1996) makes that process clear:

> American writing, it is this observer's notion, will remain without vigor until it draws upon the enormous reservoir of sick, vindictive life that moves like an underground river beneath all of our boulevards. When all the sewers back up we call it a "crime wave;" when after a while the waters subside a little we are content until the waters begin to lap the curb again. Then the pumps come out, and we're in for another wave of reforms, from press, pulpit and politician, which serve to increase newspaper circulation, fill up the pews for a few Sundays and pump up the local payrolls.[9]

Algren's use of the imagery of containment, appropriately and ironically of the sewer, highlights his concern with those boundaries of identity, for Algren was concerned with breaking down the false resolutions embedded in culture—specifically those resolutions offered by the media, church, and politics. His use of the term *sewer* is a specific one for highlighting the dissociation that occurs between the simplistic but powerful signifiers of good and bad, which blend easily into a position of "us" and "them." Of particular interest here is his attack on social reform, which in its desire to offer resolutions to problems merely becomes complicit with the perpetuation of those divisions. Although Algren's argument is fairly clear here, the rhetoric of his language reinforces a stance of absolute nonconformity that in Algren's case often merged into a perceived stance of a romantic and naive commitment to radicalism.

One of the major problems with this schema of destruction and one that haunted Benjamin and Algren similarly, is that of resolution. Both Algren and Benjamin shared a resistance to offer any absolute sense of how they would construct things differently, because they were deeply suspicious of replacing one form of power with another equally corrupt. Certainly, in the midtwentieth century the only major tangible form of oppositional political critique was that of a Marxism deeply entwined with the totalitarianism of the Soviet Union. Algren's suspicion of any form of political doctrine was one that he constantly reiterated. When questioned by H. E. F. Donohue over his politics, he replied: "I feel free to be a Marxist one day if I choose to be. *Or* an anarchist for one day." His reluctance, he argued, was his belief that "no program ever works out. You have to keep asking yourself, 'Well, is it good for the human being?' As soon as you subscribe to a definite program which is supposed to be good for all human beings, sooner or later you have to betray it."[10] That suspicion of any absolute program of change can be discerned in the ambiguities—and even contradictions—embedded in a method that deliberately sets out constantly to subvert resolutions. Algren's perceived difficulty with formal narrative structures, especially visible in the prevalence in his novels of loose episodal narratives, may be related to that fear of any form of false resolution, for Algren, like Benjamin, was a "collector" with sociological precision, moving about the ruins in order to locate and make visible the actual conditions of existence—a sociological project that did not sit comfortably with neat and tidy narratives.

The City Experience and *Never Come Morning*

The social and experiential boundaries that Algren sought to disrupt frequently corresponded with urban centers. Algren's attachment to Chicago and his relationship to urban writing, especially that of the Chicago realists, is well documented.[11] What I wish to posit here briefly is a more abstract engagement with urban writing from the work of Benjamin, which focuses on the nature of experience. For Benjamin the emergence of the modern city in the nineteenth century, particularly in Europe, produced a radical change in notions of experience and community. In his studies of those new urban centers, most notably his work on Charles Baudelaire and his massive study *The Arcades Project*, Benjamin attempted to articulate and theorize those new developments. Of particular interest to Benjamin were the "shocks" produced to individuals in the new urban centers that unsettled traditional forms of relationships: "Fear, revulsion, and horror were the emotions which the big city crowd aroused in those who first observed it."[12] The result was that the city accentuated—and physically embodied—the reifying nature of urban life and produced a bifurcation of experience, a distinction Benjamin drew between *Erlebnis*, an immediate and lived experience pertaining to a certain hour, and *Erfahrung*, an accumulated stock of integrated experience.[13] For Benjamin modern life was characterized primarily by *Erlebnis*, whereby the shocks induced by urban life—and their corollary in modes of production and consumption—induced an experience formulated on repetition and thereby limited access to any form of accumulated experience with a radical effect on community and tradition. The resultant (bourgeois) society was a fragmented mode of existence that not only resisted challenge but also substituted primarily through culture a false reconciliation of *Erlebnis* and *Erfahrung* whereby the accumulation of experience was merely illusionary.

The dynamic relationship between those two modes of experience is particularly evident in Algren's novels on Chicago and function in a manner comparable to Benjamin's analyses of urban life. Algren's urban narratives exhibit certain paradoxes and tensions that correspond in many ways to the disruptions to experience produced by the massive transformations of urban centers in the midtwentieth-century United States. Algren's characters exist in a world where they are condemned to experiences characterized primarily by repetition. The shocks of modern urban life—alienation, poverty, desperation, crime, and thwarted ambition—generate a series of experiences that are constantly grounded in the quotidian (*Erlebnis*), which constantly defers—and ultimately denies—any genuine form of cumulative or learned experience (*Erfahrung*). Each day for one of Algren's protagonists constitutes more of the same: just "getting by" and surviving.

The discrepancies between those two modes of experience are particularly evident in Algren's novel *Never Come Morning*, in which characters' experience is primarily one of repetition. An early description of the central character of the novel, Bruno "Lefty" Bicek, highlights the determining impulses of his life, "His life was a ceaseless series of lusts: for tobacco so good he could eat it like meat; for meat, for coffee, for bread, for sleep, for whiskey, for women, for dice games and ball games and personal triumphs in public places. Day and night, one or all of these rode him, and was never fully satisfied even for a while; they could no more be satisfied than they could be evaded."[14] Significantly, these desires form a confused blend of the basic necessities of life and the need for escapist pleasure. The indication here is that this "ceaseless series" creates a mode of experience in which Lefty is unable to distinguish among the various priorities in his life. The conditions of his existence are grounded in the need to satisfy *all* desires, and because none can ever be fully "satisfied" or even "evaded," even the basic necessities become conflated with addictions. Lefty is never able to achieve any kind of distance or perspective that would result from a cumulative experience and by which he could gain some control over his life. Such a circular mode of experience and the attendant lack of perspective have important implications for his self-identity. The depersonalized nature of the experience, which forms the central impulse for the narrative of the novel, is evident here. Lefty's need for recognition is again blown out of proportion—his desire is for "personal triumphs in public places"—and unable to locate securely his own identity, he pushes toward the unattainable. Lefty "was divided in his ambitions between being a big-league hurler and becoming a contender for the heavyweight championship of the world" (NCM, 11). Significantly, not only are these ambitions far beyond anything he can realistically achieve but also in his desire to be a "contender" is an implicit acknowledgment of his own fear of any ultimate resolution: even his dreams contain a grounding in a process of becoming. There is an ambiguity here in terms of conditioning, whereby he has room to maneuver, but the grounding in repetitive behavior continually defers any form of resolution.

Similarly, his desire for "women" is the depersonalized plural rather than the singular woman. The "woman" he can achieve a lasting relationship with—Steffi Rostenkowski, whom he grew up with and respects—is beyond his reach precisely because this would mean coming to terms, for Lefty, with an impossible situation. His experience is so grounded in the perpetual repetition of survival (*Erlebnis*), which he misreads as a necessary means of transcending this existence (*Erfahrung*), that it operates in an ambiguous way. By a forward movement, Lefty is driven to boxing success, to recognition that to lower his sights to the achievable would be to admit his own delusions and therefore his own identity. Moreover, the form of experience identified by Benjamin is predicated on the individual at the expense of community. When community exists in the novel it is always a fragile and conditional one that replicates the competition and gender hierarchies embedded in mainstream culture and economy. Lefty is therefore in a situation in which he is unable, or at least unwilling, to understand his relationship with Steffi: "What could you do with a good girl once she was yours?" (NCM, 36). His subsequent inaction when Steffi is gang-raped is cruelly compounded by his need for recognition by those he believes he is allowing to rape her: "This one's on me, Punchy" (NCM, 71). His justification that "Dames got to get experience just like fellas" (NCM, 70) is a flat and perverse commentary on his own relationship to experience. The violence against Steffi is indicative of the fragility of community and of the relationships built into the competitive hierarchies of gender and competition.

This dissonance between these two modes of experience is made much more explicit with the character of Casey Benkowski, who in many ways represents the person Lefty would have become had he not been arrested for murder. Casey, who is twenty-nine years old, was very much like Lefty in his teenage years but acts with no further knowledge or understanding than Lefty. Despite being knocked out in the boxing match that opens the novel, Casey nonetheless still looks to the future: "'We'll all be doin' better pretty soon, Barber,' Casey generalized, 'every time, I learn somethin' new. All the time, I'm gettin' the old experience. All the time I'm perfectin' the old technique" (NCM, 7). Casey vaguely believes he is gaining experience rather than understanding that he is merely grounded in a circularity of experience that not only is not developing but also is one of atrophy, a point emphasized only three pages later by the barber: "The boy was almost thirty, he'd been kayoed twelve times in his last fifteen fights, his strength was gone and his kidneys were gone and his heart was gone and his memory was going" (NCM, 10).

Two crucial images halfway through the novel further illustrate those ideas on experience. When Lefty is in the police cell, he dreams of his childhood and imagines back to when he was nine years old in a playground. The children were playing on a "big circular maypole: it was of iron, and had dozens of iron rings attached, to which children clung and were thus whirled in a great arc." He realizes that other children are falling off and "crashing to the gravel below," where they are killed, and he "knew then it wasn't a game after all, it was a matter of his life, and tried to cling even tighter" (NCM, 132). From the confines of his cell he becomes dimly aware of the larger societal structures that have pressed upon his life. That point is emphasized again a little later on—as a backdrop to Steffi's confinement in the brothel, where Algren moves further afield to highlight the dehumanizing nature of the city: "The world was a street like Potomac Street, with shuttered windows on either side. And only a smoldering dump at either end. All men, all women passed in darkness, like the shadows on the parlor wall, each on a separate journey. Each hurried, anxiously or eagerly, through narrowing streets to his own small and final place beside the city dump. A final place that was lightless: it was doorless and windowless too. A sign over a door would say PRIVATE, so that each could be always alone." (NCM, 194). The world beyond the novel is presented as a reflection of the situation within it, and through this, the reader is cajoled into taking a position. Of course, Algren would be aware that very few readers would actually take this as an accurate reflection of their world, and that awareness in one sense appears to be at odds with his stated aims of drawing readers into positions of responsibility. But if we bear in mind Benjamin's notions of destruction and ruin, it is possible to read a strategy whereby Algren is deliberately challenging the reader, certainly a middle-class reader, to move further away. That process would then necessitate such an alienation that, coupled with the implication that such conditions are widespread, the novel reinforces; such an absolute position of alienation is itself unsettling.

The challenge to the reader can be detected in the narrative structure—or, more accurately, the lack of structure—wherein the repetitive and often meaningless circularity of experience continually disrupts the narrative tension. In book 2, when Lefty is taken to the police station under suspicion of the shooting of a drunk, the captain is observed going over the charge sheet, "tracing the familiar menu of crime," crimes that are described as "monotonous repetitions" (NCM, 81). Throughout this chapter, the police attitude to crime almost touches on indifference. Lefty's incarceration, which takes up almost a third of the novel, is characterized by inaction, as the only form of movement occurs when the police question Lefty about his acquaintances and the crime. In those questioning sessions the reader gets very little sense that the police are actually interested in gaining any specific information, and these scenes exhibit a form of role play. The police lineup near the end of the chapter involves an almost knockabout routine wherein the captain displays his deadpan and sarcastic humor by humiliating the familiar line of usual suspects. When it is finally Lefty's turn to be questioned, the briefness of the exchange is so out of proportion to the others there is a sense that the novel has completely lost interest in Lefty. What further alienates the reader is the ambiguity concerning which crime he is specifically guilty of: the killing of the Greek, the killing of the drunk, or the crime that haunts Lefty of his allowing Steffi to be raped. Such a lack of focus, combined with the superficial narrative, unsettles the reader's attention and forces one either to search out the underlying drama or to walk away, both of which require some form of response. The emphasis on superficial experience is further evidenced by the lack of any clear sense of precise time in the novel. The interval between Steffi's rape and the killing of the Greek and Bruno's subsequent arrest for the shooting of the drunk is made evident only on page 190. Even when time is made explicit, it is given as an incidental musing by Steffi rather than having any precise relevance: "[H]ad it only been a year since the night at Riverview? It seemed like twenty" (NCM, 190).

The accumulative time in the novel bears very little relevance to the grounding in each disparate moment, and the lack of any sustained narrative tension reflects the circular notion of experience. Within this process Algren develops levels of irony wherein the dissonance between the characters and their world is mirrored by that between that of the reader and the novel. The central irony of the novel based on this form of experience—that morning never comes—is finally collapsed in the last two sentences of the novel, wherein Lefty finally realizes that he is going to be charged with murder. His response, "Knew I'd never get t' be twenty-one anyhow" (NCM, 284), is the final recognition of the futility of his existence. However, the final line taken from the boxing tournament in the background, "And the bell" (NCM, 284), renders the collapse of the irony ambiguous once more as the bell indicates both the beginning and the end of a round in boxing. The narrative continually thwarts any secure sense of development and in this way may be read as a kind of perpetually truncated bildungsroman.

This analysis of the narrative has focused on the diachronic structure, but I also think there is a synchronic element within it that may be examined through Benjamin's ideas on experience and representation. George Bluestone in his reading of the novel identified a certain tendency for the novel to produce "frozen images in which development and consciousness seem to be arrested." He then proceeds to relate this to the experiential nature of the characters in the novel: "[T]he impression of frozen life persists, as if the characters had become mere puppets, performing by role or ritual."[15] For Benjamin the purpose of critical representation and critical reading was to identify or move to a moment of crisis the contradictions inherent in the modern nature of experience. That idea revolves around the concept of "dialectics at a standstill"—a concept described by Richard Wolin as one of an "estrangement or shock-effect," which is a "game of philosophical freeze-tag in which objects are stripped of their immediacy, in order that they might be released from the sterile continuum of the always-the-same."[16] The experience of *Erlebnis* is therefore heightened to a point of crisis that is observed at certain moments to be lifted out of a narrative and displayed as stasis, a stasis moreover that shocks the reader into an understanding that the narrative is in fact an illusionary collection of those moments. Those moments of crisis reveal within them the dialectical impossibility of forward movement and therefore of any true understanding or self-realization that would accompany true accumulated experience.

The frozen images identified by Bluestone can be read as moments of a stasis that reveals a dialectical standstill. The two central chapters of *Never Come Morning*—"Only Myself to Blame" and "The Hunted Also Hope"—each display this form of stasis. In the first, Lefty is in the prison cell, where his past and future become intermingled. He dreams of a future as a boxing champion "as though he had been abruptly transplanted before a technicolor movie being reeled a little too fast" (NCM, 89). Significantly, the dream is almost involuntary and characterized by an abnormal speed that accentuates his displacement from his own situation. In the dream he is the "Modern Ketchel, resplendent in a black and red silk robe . . . contender for the heavyweight title of the world" (NCM, 89). What the dream contains are an uncanny attention to detail—"peanuts in the aisles" (NCM, 89)—and a labored description of the minutiae of the fight wherein Lefty refuses to win other than by the most noble means. There is in fact more drama, detail, and tension in the dream than in the actual situation of his arrest and questioning. This imaginary future is juxtaposed against his memories of the past—specifically, his guilt over his inaction over Steffi and the dream of the playground discussed earlier. Of course, his present situation of imprisonment completes this dialectical standstill wherein action and inaction become so entwined as to produce a moment of stasis when the thwarted energy is pushed out toward a dream state. Moreover, that dream state in its artificiality, wherein the imaginary is more real than the real, represents in distorted and accentuated form the impossibility of *any* future or cumulative experience.

A similar situation is evident in Steffi's confinement in Mama Tomek's brothel. Here the women are continually absorbed with the slot machine and the jukebox, where they "cared more for the noise the juke made in stopping and starting than for the songs it played in between" (NCM, 167). The mechanical monotony of their lives is juxtaposed against their dreams. Steffi dreams of a "man in an immaculate tuxedo with a butterfly collar . . . bending . . . formally before her" (NCM, 191). As Lefty's are, her dreams are characterized by detail, but unlike Lefty's, her dreams are quickly demolished: "[I]t was all a joke on her . . . his tuxedo was only a sleeveless blue work shirt, open at the throat" (NCM, 191). Steffi is similarly caught in a trap of perpetual repetition wherein her stasis becomes an explicit commentary on experience, but here Algren is making distinctions between levels of degradation, here along lines of gender. Significantly, in this chapter Algren makes an explicit move to the outside world and not just the transactional culpability of males but also their implicit relationship to this mode of experience, wherein the customers "dramatized their harassed, helpless, hopeless lives into gay and heroic legends of the people. And died at last, as famous as ever, beside some abandoned filling station or under the sunlit wheels" (NCM, 204). Readers who would have earlier been caught up in the drama of Lefty's dreams of heroic success are then laid with the guilt of Lefty's crime against Steffi and the implications of the relationship between their own dreams and their own existence.

Algren's fictional worlds compound and aggravate any secure sense of the relationship between the characters and their environment and indeed between the reader and the novel. One of the major characteristics of Algren's urban landscapes is claustrophobia. Scenes take place in dimly lit rooms, jails, and bars, and relationships are often fleeting or violent—a world made nebulous by Algren's frequent use of light as a means of accentuating loneliness and alienation. James R. Giles in his study of Algren's novels, *Confronting the Horror: The Novels of Nelson Algren*, explains that such a claustrophobia has the effect on the reader of creating the feeling "that no world other than that of Lefty Bicek and Frankie Machine exists because, in actuality, none does for these characters." While Giles accepts that "there is a connection between utilization of claustrophobic settings and environmental determinism," which is indicative of naturalist writing, he notes that there is also an "existential core" to Algren's best work.[17] It is this relationship between determinism and existentialism that forms a central element of Algren's writing but one that is deliberately fraught with ambiguity. While claustrophobia does in fact heighten the deterministic nature of the characters' existence, it also points toward a more-complicated disjunctive process wherein Algren appears to be searching for a position whereby he can utilize the illustrative power of both naturalism and existentialism but without collapsing into either a deterministic politics or an empty nihilism. His characters *are* victims of their material environment, but their room to maneuver is more ambiguous than determined. His characters seem always to be out of step not only with their environment but also crucially with themselves. Algren writes of Steffi that "everything was so wrong. So hopelessly and forever wrong. Always to be alone, in the wrong room always" (NCM, 244)—a condition that could be equally applicable to all of Algren's characters. Lefty's actions and nonactions are out of step: he acts to kill the Greek instead of acting to save Steffi, one of a series of misjudgments that pervade the novel. Ironically, Lefty bemoans the fact that "to be regular was all he had ever been schooled to be" (NCM, 133). His life is in fact very regular indeed, but a regularity that by its grounding in material conditions is constantly at odds with his own understanding of it. Lefty and Steffi are not necessarily determined to fail, as they do have certain agency, but neither are their actions purely devoid of content; often they act for the most noble reasons. It is this being out of step with themselves and their surroundings that is crucial and is predicated on structural conditions. However, the ambiguity and irony in Algren's work suggest an attempt to mediate between two forms of political intervention. It is a structural fault that cannot just be rectified by social reforms that seek short-term solutions; nor can it be a revolutionary transformation, which may just replace one inequitable structure for another. It appears that Algren's aim in his writing—and one he seems to have shared with Benjamin—is that the structural change should come about as much through changes in "ways of seeing" and understanding as in political programs.

Being "in the wrong room" may very well be a defining and necessary condition of the destructive character. Algren felt he was constantly at war with an unappreciative public, a greedy and manipulative publishing industry, and an exclusionary intellectual elite. I think he shared with Benjamin a frustrated sense of why other people could not see matters the same way he could. His constant battles with real and sometimes imagined enemies were indicative of a provocative writer whose intellect reaches far beyond the world of Lefty and Steffi.

Notes

1. Leslie A. Fiedler, "The Noble Savages of Skid Row," *The Reporter*, July 12, 1956, 43.

2. Maxwell Geismar, *American Moderns: From Rebellion to Conformity* (London: W. H. Allen, 1958), 187.

3. Fiedler, "The Noble Savages of Skid Row," 44.

4. Walter Benjamin, "Theses on the Philosophy of History," 245–55, in *Illuminations*, ed. Hannah Arendt, trans. Harry Zohn (1955; repr., London: Fontana, 1992), 248.

5. See especially James R. Giles, *Confronting the Horror: The Novels of Nelson Algren* (Kent, Ohio: Kent State University Press, 1989), 24–37.

6. Terry Eagleton, *Walter Benjamin or towards a Revolutionary Criticism* (London: Verso, 1981), 44.

7. Walter Benjamin, "The Destructive Character," 301–3, in *Reflections: Essays, Aphorisms, Autobiographical Writings*, ed. Peter Demetz, trans. Edmund Jephcott (New York: Schocken Books, 1978), 302-3.

8. Nelson Algren, quoted in H. E. F. Donohue, *Conversations with Nelson Algren* (New York: Hill & Wang, 1964), 94.

9. Nelson Algren, *Nonconformity: Writing on Writing* (New York: Seven Stories Press, 1996), 35.

10. Algren, quoted in Donohue, *Conversations with Nelson Algren*, 257.

11. In particular, Carla Cappetti, *Writing Chicago: Modernism, Ethnography, and the Novel* (New York: Columbia University Press, 1993), and Carlo Rotella, *October Cities: The Redevelopment of Urban Literature* (Berkeley: University of California Press, 1998).

12. Walter Benjamin, *Charles Baudelaire: A Lyric Poet in the Era of High Capitalism*, trans. Harry Zohn (London: New Left Books, 1973), 121.

13. Ibid., 117. See also Richard Wolin, *Walter Benjamin: An Aesthetics of Redemption* (New York: Columbia University Press, 1982), 213–49.

14. Nelson Algren, *Never Come Morning* (1942; repr., New York: Seven Stories Press, 1996), 31. Further references are to this edition and are cited parenthetically as NCM.

15. George Bluestone, "Nelson Algren," *Western Review* 22 (1957): 31–33.

16. Wolin, *Walter Benjamin,* 125.

17. Giles, *Confronting the Horror,* 20.

Spatial Enclosures in Nelson Algren's *Never Come Morning*

Robert Ward

In an article that is now considered seminal in Nelson Algren scholarship, George Bluestone reads *Never Come Morning* (1942) as "a series of frozen images in which development and consciousness seem to be arrested."[1] The reading is important not only because it was one of the first serious critical surveys of Algren's work but also as it—perhaps unintentionally—scratches the surface of certain nuances of confinement that inform the setting and characterization of the novel. "[F]rozen" and "arrested" are its key conceptual terms of engagement, and they highlight the static atmosphere said to be circumscribing the ghettoized rituals of Chicago's Northwest Side. Consequently, the social processes that transfer the "delinquent" individual from the streets to the prisons—what James Spradley sees as the "revolving door" of ghetto existence—are rendered transparent.[2] But Bluestone's terms, although establishing a consensual view of Algren's work, are not absolutes. Rather, they imply and demand opposites, such as, to start with, *thawed* and *escape*. It is my interest in these "opposites" that guides the following discussion.

The City

Using a critical framework similar to Bluestone's, Mary Ellen Pitts translates the elevated-train network in Chicago into a narrative device that connects the city and the prison. Here the metallic architecture of the El train, with its "heavy, regular, riveted beams," is extended in order to forge comparisons with the high walls and steel bars that visually define a penal landscape. From both environments, writes Pitts, "there is no escape."[3]

The argument is appealing and is clearly supported by the fact that characters rarely leave their Division Street neighborhood. In the few instances that the novel's hero, Bruno "Lefty" Bicek, does leave—such as his participation with the Warriors Social and Athletic Club in a robbery of an out-of-town grocery store—we are told that he experiences "a pang of anticipation" (NCM, 20). The anxiety of being outside the boundaries of gangland territory—what Carla Cappetti suggests is "literally abroad for the neighborhood youths"—certainly exposes a register of that entrapment.[4]

At the same time as I support that view, its very thesis is haunted by contexts that, although not exactly ignored, have their importance mislaid. I want to suggest, then, that in order to engage appropriately with Algren's re-presentation of urban and penal landscapes, particular "hidden" and "enclosed" spaces should be reexamined with a different and more penetrating lens. My intention is not to explicate the naturalistic *style* that is said to invest Algren's writing but, rather, to identify issues that cross into an aesthetic of imprisonment.

A useful place to start is with the characterization of Bicek, which is developed more "beneath the shadow" (NCM, 29) of the city than on its surface. Within that "hidden" and "private" space, Bicek mentally constructs "a wall between himself and the world" (NCM, 31). This appears to lend itself to the views of Bluestone and Pitts were it not for the peculiarities of such scenes, for Bicek is not passive but, rather, identifies areas of the city that remind him of "the warmth and security of the womb" (NCM, 31), which he then actively uses to produce an image of himself as "a rejuvenated Adam" (NCM, 48). What occurs in between those sequences represents an attempt to cultivate what David Theodore Boxer calls the "iron triangle"[5] of the Chicago ghetto into spaces pregnant with possibility.

One of the most seminal anthropological studies of that "iron triangle" and the gangs existing within it is, of course, Frederic M. Thrasher's work *The Gang: A Study of 1,313 Gangs in Chicago,* published in 1927. Introducing this book some twenty years later, and with Thrasher's "observations" clearly in mind, the Chicago sociologist Robert E. Park suggested that "solitary persons . . . establish intimate relationships with their physical environment and find 'sermons in stones, books in running brooks.'"[6] That paradigm of solitude, which reflects the ways in which the isolated individual reads and imaginatively reconstructs the surrounding environment, lends a provocative insight into the nature of Bicek. The following passage from *Never Come Morning* offers a good example of it: "The single-car local to Humboldt Park slowed up overhead and clattered lamely west; to the boy's ears the clatter became a crescendo of applause. He jabbed with his right and threw the left—that's the hand they were cheering. A right to the heart and a left to the jaw. He bobbed, ducked, covered, swung and straightened up: the applause was faint and far away and then it was gone" (NCM, 37). This "daydream" echoes the "intimate" connection to the urban landscape evoked by Park. Here the animation of Bicek's physical gestures, together with the "crescendo of applause" that celebrates his presence and aspirations as a boxer, is shaped by the surrounding soundscape of the El.

Algren's use of daydreams, then, relies on spaces "hidden" from public view: the "underground" tunnels beneath the city streets, the areas situated within the metallic framework of the El, and the prison cell "in an abandoned corner of the basement" (NCM, 87). Pitts does not consider this perspective from "below," but it is, I would argue, fundamental in reconfiguring the bases of the character's development. Gaston Bachelard's *The Poetics of Space* is grounded on the same idea: "Immensity is within ourselves. It is attached to a sort of expansion of being that life curbs and caution arrests, but which starts again when we are alone. As soon as we become motionless, we are elsewhere; we are dreaming in a world that is immense. Indeed, immensity is the movement of motionless man. It is one of the dynamic characteristics of quiet daydreaming."[7] The passage touches and extends the aura of what Maxwell Geismar calls the "iron sanctuary"[8] in *Never Come Morning* and precipitates the "movement" to "elsewhere." The "immensity" that such spaces evoke is part of Algren's protest aesthetic, which he picked up during the political radicalism of the 1930s and which reveals what Angela Davis calls the "vicious circle linking poverty, police, courts and prisons [which] is an integral part of ghetto existence."[9]

Drawing out this same perspective as stimulated "underground," Algren also uses the "over-ground" platform of the Ferris wheel to invest his character with a near-omniscient perspective of the city: "He forced himself to look: thousands of little people and hundreds of bright little stands, and over it all the coal-smoke pall of the river factories and railroad yards. He saw in that moment the whole dim-lit city on the last night of summer; the troubled streets that led to the abandoned beaches, the for-rent signs above overnight hotels and furnished basement rooms, moving trolleys and rising bridges: the cagework city, beneath a coal-smoke sky" (NCM, 61–62). As in the "underground" spaces, Bicek is no longer caught up in the ghetto but distanced from it. It is that distance that enables him to map the paths that lead from erosion and sterility (defined by the "troubled streets . . . abandoned beaches, [and] coal-smoke pall") into the moving parts of the city (a landscape of "moving trolleys and rising bridges"). In charting those routes, the quest for more-dynamic spaces of possibility and empowerment is established.

In *The Practice of Everyday Life*—a discussion that introduces telescopic views of New York from the top of the World Trade Center—Michel de Certeau touches on the implications of such a vision; "His elevation transfigures him into a voyeur. It puts him at a distance. It transforms the bewitching world by which one was 'possessed' into a text that lies before one's eyes. It allows one to read it, to be a solar Eye, looking down like a god."[10] It is interesting to consider Bicek as a "solar Eye." Through such a lens, we glimpse the strength and vision of the character that Algren wants us to see—in order to expose the rationale of a system that by the end of the novel finally succeeds in killing both the dream and the individual.

This is the "vicious circle," outlined by Davis earlier, inextricably associated with juvenile delinquency. The gang, which Bicek has been a member of since an early age, is called the "26th Ward Warriors S.A.C." Because of its associations with criminality, very likely Bicek was a member of the gang at the age of fourteen, when he spent two nights in a prison cell for assault. Consequently, he becomes further alienated from his first-generation Polish mother, who feels ashamed of her son's behavior: "Fourteen years old and he had thought nothing of being two days in a jail. She had taken no pleasure in him since" (NCM, 16).

It is that separation from a Polish heritage and an older generation, together with the feeling of being ostracized from "mainstream" American society ("people who lived in houses" [NCM, 29]), that makes the gang familial. A similar "unconscious" appeal exists in Richard Wright's *Native Son* (1940). Here the family of Bigger Thomas displays a crude but real understanding of the gang and its delinquent activities, which, especially for young black men, leads almost inevitably to imprisonment.

It is certainly true that as James R. Giles suggests, the Warriors are "trapped within a suffocating existence,"[11] but Bicek does seek out such an existence, at least temporarily, in the same way as he occupies and uses particular urban and institutional spaces. As mentioned earlier, Thrasher conducted one of the most comprehensive studies of the gang during the mid-1920s. His analysis became one of the cornerstones of sociological studies of gangs, their ethnicities, and the often-impoverished neighborhoods in which they operate. Although the book is informed by social science, Thrasher does include some rather provocative observations—for example, "the gang boy transform[s] his sordid environment through his imagination."[12] Algren studied sociology and criminology under Donald Taft in the late 1920s and would have almost certainly come across this passage in Thrasher, which he would later translate into the characterization of Bicek. Thus, we see the character imaginatively transform the littered alleyways into a boxing ring where he is "carried away . . . by his own possibilities" (NCM, 47).

Although he is physically caught within a landscape blighted by urban degeneration, we still see Bicek—in the same way as we see James T. Farrell's Studs Lonigan—moving through his constructed "other" world. Thrasher again: "He sees in a broken sewer a sea on which sails the Spanish Armada. A sour basement becomes an ogre's cave; a dank areaway, a glorified castle. To him the piles of rubbish in the city dumps or the mud hills along the drainage canal are mountain fastnesses, while stretches of wasteland become prairies of the Golden West."[13] The flight of the imagination that Thrasher alludes to works from a similar aura of solitude and enclosure as the space of "elsewhere" proposed by Bachelard. In both studies, the human image that ultimately arises—Thrasher's by the probability of incarceration in the gang member's lifetime and Bachelard's in his view of Gustave Courbert's painting the "unseen" urban landscape from his dungeon—is that of the prisoner in a cell. It is from that particular context that Bicek's question—"What am I—Superman?" (NCM, 19)—is given a validity that not only allows him to survive imprisonment but also to foresee his future triumph as a contender for the world heavyweight boxing crown. It is to that particular context, then, that I now turn my attention.

The Prison Cell

In what follows I address a scene in *Never Come Morning* that presents the world title bout enacted mentally by Bicek while imprisoned in a police holding cell. As in the isolated spaces underneath the landscape of Chicago, it is a narrative of rejuvenation and empowerment as much as it is an experience of entrapment and regulation. In the context of imprisonment, then, Bicek actively exploits the link between the cell and the "warmth and security of the womb" (NCM, 31) by becoming fetal: "bent above his berth, his hands folded in his forearms and his forearms on his knees" (NCM, 96).

Such a relationship, drawn between the prison cell and the freedom of the prisoner, must appear paradoxical. The implication that the prison is, in Theodore Dreiser's words, "horrible—something like a living tomb," informs our reading of those environments and cannot be ignored,[14] but the idea of the cell as stimulating—what W. B. Carnochan calls "the multiplicity of human possibility and experience"—exists symbiotically in cultural representations of imprisonment: an aesthetic that Algren crosses into and uses.[15] The paradox or glitch is part of this and is used by Algren to undermine the boundaries of a discourse (which Michel Foucault labels "the instrument and vector of power"[16]) that defines and justifies socioeconomic and penal systems in contemporary America.

Algren constructs such a thematic of solitude around the senses of the prisoner. Thus, Bicek "had been placed in an abandoned corner of the basement," and within that setting "he realized he was alone" (NCM, 87). Here he begins "pacing the cell's gray length" (NCM, 88) "up and down" (NCM, 86), thereby augmenting the claustrophobic feel, as well as the proscriptions on physical movement. Only a few steps are taken in any direction before one confronts walls and bars, and because of this "up and down" linearity, the terrible immediacy of confinement and its omniscient surveillance of the body are imbued in the consciousness of the inmate.

However, the interrelations among confinement, surveillance, and regulation of action that define the rationale of the penal system become inverted as Bicek's "mind was swamped by an image of himself; as though he had been abruptly transplanted before a technicolor movie being reeled a little too fast" (NCM, 88–89). The very beginning of the daydream, then, is reflected in a language that jars with our understanding of the prison. In this moment, the character no longer sees the cell as background and foreground to his body. Instead, as in the landscape underneath the El frame, Bicek notices only "an image of himself," which has been removed from the institutional setting and "abruptly transplanted" into Bachelard's space of "elsewhere." Although still physically situated within the small, silent, and monochromatic cell, he also experiences the "stirring drama of . . . the vast park" (NCM, 89), with all of its associated noises, smells, and colors.

Colors also figure in the appearance of the inmate. At the time of imprisonment, he "was wearing a worn and sleeveless blue work shirt, grown too tight across the shoulders," along with "a pair of faded corduroys, tennis shoes grown dirt-gray from snow, and a pavement-colored cap" (NCM, 80). This detail shows Bicek as being clothed in the same nondescript tonality as the prison cell itself. But the image is shattered by the daydream, in which he sees himself "resplendent in a black and red silk robe" his body "in perfect trim and freshly tanned" (NCM, 89). The words *resplendent* and *perfect* remove Bicek from gangland adolescence into a statuesque version of the superman who appropriates and subordinates space in order to realize the aspirations of the self. And he searches for names that would reflect that change: rather than passive Bruno "Lefty" Bicek, he will be "Bombshell Bicek" or "Superman Bicek." He finally settles for "Powerhouse Bicek, the Modern Ketchel" (NCM, 89). These titles fix the self in this dynamic and ideal "elsewhere," and in so doing, explode the rigid parameters of penality that function to constrain the prisoner.

The conflict investing the descriptions of colors, names, and settings exposes what Henri Lefebvre would call "an uprising of the body . . . against the signs of non-body"—the latter inextricably associated with the historical nature of the prison system in America.[17] As the term *uprising* suggests, the actions of Bicek signify a form of resistance against any system that inhibits the potential of the self. The imagined space, then, becomes, in de Certeau's words, "a space of enunciation" because it hides an entire landscape from the surveillance of the prison.[18] We see the actual physical body of the prisoner weaving around the cell, using the concrete floor as the canvas of the ring and the walls as its ropes. The semiotics of this "performance" mark an "opening-out" of the prison's one-dimensional essence—to confine—as a means to attain a vision of individual empowerment and liberation.

In the context of this imagined space, Bicek, despite "weighing in" at "195-pound," is light, as if he is almost floating over the ropes. Even in the ring, he returns "lightly to his corner in a flutter of red and black" (NCM, 89). The associations of weightlessness and flight are difficult to ignore here, especially when set against the physical heaviness of confinement that holds prisoners "like the weight upon them of an incurable disease" (NCM, 86).

In *Society of Captives: A Study of a Maximum Security Prison*, Gresham M. Sykes observes that "like a body of stream . . . the body of prisoners are limited in modes of adaptation."[19] And narratives of lightness and mental flight underscore these modes, as displayed in such prison novels as Jack London's *Star Rover* (1915) and, here, *On the Yard* (1967), written by Malcolm Braly (still one of the most important yet undervalued prison writers of the twentieth century). Here the character Creepy is seen in his cell gazing into space. His mind, though, is *elsewhere*: "He flew out over the prison above the solid square heart of interlocking cellblocks, over the cream stucco and red tile of the education building, where in another incarnation he had once worked, he passed along the length of the old industrial building and around the walls that closed in the lower yard."[20] Here, quite literally, the entire landscape of the penitentiary is being subordinated to the flight of the "I," in a single moment of contemplation. This, then, is a narrative of escape—because the flight transgresses the boundaries constructed to confine—as it is for Bicek's mapping of other spaces from the Ferris wheel, the underground tunnels, and, ultimately, the prison cell.

Erving Goffman refers to such "daydreams"—specifically in the context of institutional culture—as "removal activities" that "lift the participant out of himself."[21] It is both the idea of "dreams of flight" and the feeling of being lifted "out of himself" that are of interest here because they are configured as forms of resistance, constantly pushing the boundaries surrounding and regulating the inmate. In "Social Control in the Prison," Richard A. Cloward sees such resistance as a reaction to the "ritual destruction of the individual's identity," which underpins the historical rationale of the penal system in America. The prisoner's acute sense of degradation (a trait that Algren invests in all of his key characters), he says serves to "generate powerful pressures to evolve means of restoring [or, in Bicek's case, creating] status."[22]

In order to augment the physicality of this "performance," which is shaped by the simulacrum of the boxing ring, we are never allowed to forget that the body of the character dances around the cell. As Bicek is seen "leaping the top strand lightly" in one context, then, he still "turned on his ankle in the cell coming down" (NCM, 89). If we play down the imagined landscape of the dream for a moment and spotlight this purely physical spectacle confronting the guards, then the tension between the institutional system and the individual—"an uprising of the body . . . against the signs of non-body"—becomes fully exposed.

The same symbolism can be found in other "bottom-dog" (prison/boxing) narratives (the category is never wholly suitable). It exists in the book *Raging Bull: My Story* (1970), for example, during a scene that involves Jake La Motta being removed from the general inmate population and placed in solitary confinement; "Maybe it was my fighting instinct, my survival instinct, I don't know—all I knew was the fucking system, whatever it was that had shoved me into this hole, was not going to have the last say. . . . And the wall closest to me became the whole stinking world. I doubled my fists tight and lashed out at it, at them. I hit them where it hurt—in the gut, in the windpipe, on the chin."[23] The power of the prison—and by inference the socioeconomic system built around it—is visualized in terms of the vulnerable parts of an opponent's body while in the ring: "[T]he gut . . . windpipe . . .

chin" are impressed as inscriptions are upon the wall of the cell. The same can be said about *Never Come Morning*, as Bicek "drove a left to the heart and a right to the jaw" directly in front of the cell wall. Despite being physically injured, La Motta realizes that the confrontation has helped him beat the fear—the same "fear" that Bicek "brushed . . . aside" (NCM, 94), which had been an obstacle to personal fulfillment. As a result, "There was only one way to go now, and that was UP."[24]

Such choreography celebrates the boxer, who embodies what Gerald Early calls "the enormous possibility of true meaning, the incendiary poetics, of actual self-determination."[25] For the boxer, the "knockout" is the ultimate translation of freedom, the explosion of "incendiary poetics," and a catalyst for the rapid empowerment of the self. In *Never Come Morning*, the imagined—and prophetic—act of knocking out the "heavyweight champion of the universe!" (NCM, 94) draws on all of these experiences. The terminus of the dream match plays on our expectations of the sight of the fighter, arms lifted in a gesture of victory, as occurs in the final scene of the book. The gesture, occurring in both the "fictional" landscape of "the roped arena" (NCM, 92) and the literal site of the cell, also tentatively evokes the fugitive movements associated with the newly escaped prisoner. *The Shawshank Redemption* (1994) (Frank Darabont's cinematic pastiche of the clichés inherent to a prison aesthetic) also plays on this connection by following Andy Dufresne as he crawls through the waste pipe to freedom: "He raises his arms to the sky, turning slowly, feeling the rain washing him clean. Exultant. Triumphant. A FLASH OF LIGHTNING arcs from horizon to horizon."[26] The elevation of the arms—mirroring the final hieroglyphic of the fight—signifies the liberation and, even, the salvation of the individual. For Bicek, viewing such a totemic image of himself, this inevitably leads to hubris, something that drives him to reenact the vision in reality.

Toward the Final Scene

After being sentenced to the penitentiary on a nine-month "misdemeanor," Bicek experiences firsthand the appalling conditions that drive some prisoners to the point of insanity. With very little else to do, he spends his time listening to "the sounds of human trouble" (NCM, 153) that echo throughout the institution. After seven months of this sentence, though, there is a marked transformation of the character. The daydreams that he enacts in the various spaces of enclosure throughout urban and institutional landscapes—together with the empowering graffiti that he scores on the wall of his cell—are translated on the "outside" into a card that announces his ambition and strength to the world (NCM, 234):

> Bruno Lefty Biceps
> contender for the heavyweight championship
> of the world
> Conqueror of Greek Christophor, Vincent Guerra, Turkey Johnson,
> Ink Martin, Nash Cooney, etc., etc.
>
> Casey Benkowski, Magr. Finger Idzikowski, Trainer

The card is significant in that it affirms an opportunity for Bicek to realize his dream of, and potential for, becoming a world-ranking prizefighter. As a result of the new manager and former boxer Casey Benkowski's arranging a fight against Honey Boy Tucker, we are told that even the young characters of the gang were "bursting with pride" (NCM, 234). For the first time in his life, Bicek has an absolute faith in himself and is able to tell Steffi "with no shade of doubt in his mind" that he has become an unbeatable contender for the world heavyweight crown (NCM, 256).

When Bicek eventually steps into the ring to fight Tucker, he is introduced as "the great new contenda fer the heavyweight champeen" (NCM, 261). The extent of Bicek's transformation is affirmed after he is knocked onto the canvas by Tucker. It is only here that "He looked around hopelessly, searching for that Bruno B. with one eye. But Bruno B. was in jail" (NCM, 274). The boxer standing in the ring confronting Tucker, then, is a "new man," and this awareness inspires him to deliver the knockout punch that signals victory.

Again, the force of the punch reverberates with echoes of escape, a "break-out" from institutional enclosures: "It hit something that felt as though he'd driven his hand through a wooden wall," causing "A falling away, a crumbling" (NCM, 279). Benkowski's suggestion that "two more like that 'n they'll give you the big fella" (NCM, 281) verifies this sense of release for Bicek himself, who experiences "the full realization that, at last, he had won" (NCM, 282). The fact that he is arrested again—this time for the murder of "a Greek" (NCM, 80)—does little to undermine the initial vision of the new contender—and of his strength in having articulated it in reality. Bicek has won the final bell. This in mind, Jeffrey T. Sammons's study of the fighter in American culture becomes an endnote pertinent to *Never Come Morning*; "He is the embodiment of the American Dream, in which the lowliest individuals rise to the top by their own initiative and perseverance. The elusiveness of that dream is immaterial; the meaning of the dream is in its acceptance, not its fulfillment."[27]

Notes

1. George Bluestone, "Nelson Algren," *Western Review* 22 (1957): 31.

2. James Spradley, *You Owe Yourself a Drunk: An Ethnography of Urban Nomads* (Boston: Little, Brown, 1970), 66. The passage in full reads: "At worst, they're treated like criminals scooped up by the bum wagon, hauled into court . . . then tossed back to the street to be swept up again in what amounts to a revolving door."

3. Mary Ellen Pitts, "Algren's El: Internalized Machine and Displaced Nature," *South Atlantic Review* 52 (1987): 63. *Never Come Morning* (1942; repr., London: Fourth Estate, 1988), 31. Further references are to this edition and are cited parenthetically as NCM.

4. Carla Cappetti, *Writing Chicago: Modernism, Ethnography and the Novel* (New York: Columbia University Press, 1993), 160.

5. David Theodore Boxer, "Social Allegory in the Novels of Nelson Algren" (Ph.D. dissertation, University of Washington, 1970), 68.

6. Robert E. Park, preface to *The Gang: A Study of 1,313 Gangs in Chicago*, by Frederic M. Thrasher (1927; repr., Chicago: University of Chicago Press, 1947), x.

7. Gaston Bachelard, *The Poetics of Space*, trans. Maria Jolas (1964; repr., Boston: Beacon Press, 1994), 184.

8. Maxwell Geismar, *American Moderns: From Rebellion to Conformity* (New York: Hill & Wang, 1958), 187.

9. Angela Y. Davis, *If They Come in the Morning: Voices of Resistance* (London: Orbach and Chambers, 1971), 39. Although Davis was using the cyclical model to explore the complexities of black urban existence, it is nevertheless clearly appropriate for an understanding of ghetto life generally.

10. Michel de Certeau, *The Practice of Everyday Life*, trans. Steven Rendall (1984; repr., Berkeley: University of California Press, 1988), 92.

11. James R. Giles, *Confronting the Horror: The Novels of Nelson Algren* (Kent, Ohio: Kent State University Press, 1989), 46.

12. Thrasher, *The Gang*, 117.

13. Ibid., 116.

14. Theodore Dreiser, *The Financier* (1912; repr., New York: Thomas Y. Crowell, 1974), 442.

15. W. B. Carnochan, "The Literature of Confinement," 381–406, in *The Oxford History of the Prison: The Practice of Punishment in Western Society*, ed. Norval Morris and David J. Rothman (Oxford: Oxford University Press, 1998), 403.

16. Michel Foucault, *Discipline and Punish: The Birth of the Prison*, trans. Alan Sheridan (1971; repr., Harmondsworth, England: Penguin, 1991), 30.

17. Henri Lefebvre, *The Production of Space*, trans. Donald Nicholson-Smith (1991; repr., Oxford: Blackwell, 1995), 201.

18. de Certeau, *The Practice of Everyday Life*, 98.

19. Gresham M. Sykes, *The Society of Captives: A Study of a Maximum Security Prison* (Princeton, N.J.: Princeton University Press, 1968), 79.

20. Malcolm Braly, *On the Yard* (1967; repr., Harmondsworth, England: Penguin, 1977), 49. For more information on Braly see his autobiography, *False Starts: A Memoir of San Quentin and Other Prisons* (Harmondsworth, England: Penguin, 1976). H. Bruce Franklin also includes a critical survey of Braly's work in *Prison Literature in America: The Victim as Criminal and Artist*, rev. ed. (Oxford: Oxford University Press, 1989).

21. Erving Goffman, "On the Characteristics of Total Institutions: The Inmate World," 15–67, in *The Prison: Studies in Institutional Organization and Change*, ed. Donald R. Cressey (New York: Holt, Rinehart & Winston, 1961), 63.

22. Richard A. Cloward, "Social Control in the Prison," 20–48, in *Theoretical Studies in Social Organization of the Prison*, ed. Richard A. Cloward, et al. (New York: Social Science Research Council, 1960), 20, 21.

23. Jake La Motta, with Joseph Carter and Peter Savage, *Raging Bull: My Story* (1970; repr., New York: Da Capo Press, 1997), 206.

24. Ibid., 208.

25. Gerald Early, "Tales of a Wonderboy," introduction to *I'm a Little Special: A Muhammad Ali Reader*, ed. Gerald Early (London: Yellow Jersey Press, 1999), xiv.

26. Frank Darabont, *The Shooting Script: The Shawshank Redemption* (London: Nick Hern Books, 1996), 103.

27. Jeffrey T. Sammons, *Beyond the Ring: The Role of Boxing in American Society* (Urbana: University of Illinois Press, 1990), 3.

Detachment, Compassion, and Irritability: The Naturalism of *Never Come Morning*

Kasia Boddy

THE QUESTION MOST OFTEN RAISED ABOUT NELSON ALGREN'S WORK is its relation to naturalism.[1] In this essay, I follow tradition, although with an eye less on the often-discussed issues of determinism and the city than on the complexities of authorial stance; my aim is to consider Algren's ambitions toward (various forms of) detachment alongside his impulse toward (various forms of) engagement. I consider what the tensions, or indeed contradictions, between those positions entail for the fiction itself by focusing on Algren's second novel, *Never Come Morning* (1942).

In a 1955 interview for the *Paris Review,* Algren formulated a variety of responses when questioned about authorial stance and tone. When asked whether he felt he needed to try heroin in order to write about users, he replied, "No, I think you can do a thing like that best from a detached position."[2] Later, however, when Malcolm Cowley tried to link him with his near contemporary and fellow Chicago chronicler James T. Farrell, Algren objected, complaining that Farrell was "too journalistic," "I don't get anything besides a social study. . . . It isn't enough to do just a case study, something stenographic. Farrell is stenographic, and he isn't even a real good stenographer. . . . In his essays he compares himself with Dreiser, but I don't think he's in Dreiser's league. He's as *bad* a writer as Dreiser—but he doesn't have the compassion that makes Dreiser's bad writing important."[3]

Compassion here is contrasted with the detachment of mere stenography. A few pages later, a third possible stance is introduced. Algren was asked whether he could relate *The Man with the Golden Arm* (1949) to "an idea." "No," he replied, "unless a feeling can be an idea."

> I just had an over-all *feeling*, I didn't have any particular theory about what I ought to do. Living in a very dense area, you're conscious of how the people underneath live, and you have a certain feeling toward them—so much so that you'd rather live among them than with the business classes. In a historical sense, it might be related to an idea, but you write out of—well, I wouldn't call it indignation, but a kind of *irritability* that these people on top should be so contented, so absolutely unaware of these other people, and so sure that their values are the right ones. I mean, there's a certain satisfaction in recording the people underneath, whose values are as sound as theirs, and a lot funnier, and a lot truer in a way. There's a certain over-all satisfaction in kind of scooping up a shovelful of these people and dumping them in somebody's parlor.[4]

After "detachment" and "compassion," then, are "irritability," and finally the "over-all satisfaction" of "scooping up" and "dumping" his characters into the parlors of the privileged and the proper.

Never Come Morning is set during the Depression in Chicago's Little Polonia, an area bounded by three streets—Chicago, Ashland, and Milwaukee avenues—and referred to as "the Triangle."[5] It tells the story of Bruno Bicek, a young boxer-turned-hoodlum, and Steffi, his girlfriend-turned-prostitute, as they struggle with the encroaching forces of the neighborhood. A reader picking up the novel today will encounter two statements before the story begins. The first is an epigraph from Walt Whitman's poem "You Felons on Trial in Courts":

> I feel I am of them—I belong to those convicts and
> prostitutes myself,
> And henceforth I will not deny them—for how can
> I deny myself?[6]

The second is an "Author's Preface," which Algren added in 1962, largely in response to the negative reception his novel had received from the Polish press in Chicago: "Yet the novel that so infuriated them . . . was nothing more than a thinly fictionalized report on a neighborhood. . . . The book drew for its details not upon the after-effects of a narcotic jag but upon the lives of half a dozen men with whom the writer had grown up, as well as upon the newspaper reports of the trial of Bernard 'Knifey' Sawicki" (NCM, preface, xv).[7] I want to start by considering what each of these statements suggests the method of the novel will be.

The Whitman epigraph seems to instruct the reader that the book's mode will be one of empathy or even identification, that no distinction between the writer and his subject will exist: "I am of them." In the later preface, Algren quotes those lines again, concluding that the "failure of the people at Polish newspaper *Zgoda* was a failure of feeling. A failure to feel 'I am of them . . . [etc.]' " (NCM, preface, xvi). This seems straightforward enough, but two questions arise: The first is factual—Is total identification really the case, with either Whitman or Algren? And the second is more theoretical: Assuming it were the case, what would the implications be for their writing?

Rolf Lindner argues for the importance of Whitman for the Chicago school of sociology and in particular, the work of Robert E. Park, who taught at the School of Journalism where Algren studied. Whitman, Lindner claims, was "the spiritual founding father of the romantic interest in human diversity, which was at the same time based on an underlying democratic impulse."[8] Whitman certainly announced the centrality of inclusiveness to the project of *Leaves of Grass* (1855) in his preface: "The American bard shall delineate no class of persons nor one or two out of the strata of interests"—and, with what might be seen as a protosociological impartiality, poems such as "Song of Myself" refuse discrimination at all points.[9] "Wickedness" and "goodness," "the hounded slave" and "the slave driver," are presented with the same syntactical, and moral, weight.[10]

But Whitman is not strictly accurate when he says he shall "delineate no class of persons" above the rest, for one class does receive special attention: "the American bard," who speaks *for* the American masses as much as *of* them. So while Whitman asserted that he was "no stander above men and women or apart from them," he also claimed that "I act as the tongue of you, / It was tied in your mouth . . . in mine it begins to be loosened." Indeed he ended "Song of Myself" by saying he was "waiting for you," his readers, to follow.[11]

The Whitmanesque conundrum (being of them, or speaking for them) persists in Algren's early writing—most explicitly in a series of poems in which, his biographer Bettina Drew argues, he first articulated his writerly persona. In one poem, Algren wrote:

> I can speak for you better
> Than you can for yourself. . . .

In other words, as is Whitman, he is "better," at least at speaking for others, than "you" are, and this "you" seems to be universal. Yet in another poem, Algren rejected that universalism, claiming, "Being a loser I speak only for losers." Precisely delineated identification is now the key to speech.[12] He is not speaking for or embracing all; rather, selection (of losers) precedes compassion.

In *Nonconformity: Writing on Writing* (1996), Algren quoted a passage from F. Scott Fitzgerald's "The Crack-Up" about the dangerous consequences of identification. Pondering why "I had become identified with objects of my horror or compassion," Fitzgerald had concluded that "identification such as this spells the death of accomplishment."[13] One way of reading *Never Come Morning* is as a novel about the dangers, but also about the inevitability, of such identification. I want to focus on one scene in which this is made very clear: the final chapter of book one, "The Trouble with Bicek." The titles of the previous two chapters signal an interest in other forms of "the trouble"—first with the barber, the novel's villain, and then with daylight. "The Trouble with Bicek" is the pivotal chapter of the novel; the events that occur there determine the course of the rest, the course of Bruno's and Steffi's lives. The parallel titles of these three chapters seem, however, to suggest that there are three causes (three troubles): most directly, Casey, the barber, is responsible, and then Bruno himself, but a third factor, "daylight," the "morning" of the book's title—and a metaphor of the real—also dooms the protagonists.

Algren uses a series of urban spaces in the novel—the boxing ring, the brothel, the gang clubhouse, the poolroom, the barber shop (and the birdcage within it), the police station, and the amusement park—to create a network of symbols of enclosure, and that network is continually reinforced by a use of light and dark imagery that recalls contemporary noir fiction and film. In the symbolic lexicon of noir, their meanings are straightforward: artificial light distorts and disguises; authenticity, honesty, reality are possible only in glimpses of daylight. For Bruno, "Sunlight and daytime were hostile things" (NCM, 29).

"The Trouble with Bicek" does not feature daylight; the chapter begins in the evening as Bruno and Steffi walk toward the main gate at Riverview Park. He is taking her there to "make it up to her" after effectively raping her in the previous chapter (NCM, 29). "The gate had a million lights, and he sensed her excitement: each light was burning for Steffi R. tonight" (NCM, 51). "Making it up" or compensating is a recurrent motive of the passage and, indeed, the book, but as we shall see, compensation is often associated with artificiality.

Steffi and Bruno start with the freak show and pass the cages of creatures (another image of enclosure), but the animals are not only imprisoned but also stuffed. "I wanna see somethin' alive" (NCM, 52), Bruno says. He then bats a baseball (while dreaming that he's playing the Yankees) and wins Steffi a Kewpie doll. She loves it (she has never had a doll), but soon—frustrated that he's not "a man in the world of men," but with "a thin girl called Steffi hugging a Kewpie and calling him Bunny as though it were a baby and he was too"—he rips off the doll's head. Immediately and characteristically, he is repentant and again wants to "make it up to" her. First he offers an explanation: "I didn't like seein' you hold'n' onto a dummy like it was a real kid, it made you look like a dummy too. I don't want my girl to be no dummy. That makes a dummy out of me." There is a rather odd transference of identity going on here. Clutching a fake child makes you a fake woman; clutching a fake woman makes you a fake man. Steffi tells him she does not feel like a dummy, and "What I think is you need a steady job." He ignores this and tells her, "I don't feel like no dummy when I'm pitchin' 'r scrappin', Steff," as if sport rather than a steady job represents the real. She concurs, "We both want live things—*Don't* we, Bunny?" (NCM, 54–55). But do they?

The pattern of this initial interaction between them—on Bruno's part, a pattern of good intentions, frustration that leads to violence, and a desire to make up—is played out several more times in the chapter and both repeats and foreshadows the pattern of other chapters. George Bluestone has described the novel's structure as "a series of frozen images in which development and consciousness seem to be arrested"; more than that, however, the very receptiveness of imagery and scene underscores Algren's preoccupation with stasis.[14] Bruno and Steffi drink some beer, and she flatters and excites him by making him show her his pitching skills. Algren describes their increasing sexual excitement as "Skyrockets began bursting a thousand miles overhead": "She began drawing in her breath, once her reverence had passed, in sharp, dreamy little hisses, her underlip caught between her teeth. He felt her very breathing exciting him. The thought broke over him like another man's idea: 'Get some liquor in her. That's what dames are for' (NCM, 57). A complex series of unmediated and mediated responses is presented here. First, we have Steffi's "very breathing"—a direct physical response. This is followed by Bruno's awareness of his excitement and realization that it is caused by her breathing. Steffi just feels; Bruno feels himself feeling. For Bruno, there is no experience (authentic or inauthetic) without mediation. Even before a "dummy thing" once more intrudes—a "thought . . . like another man's idea"—authenticity is already seen to include reflectiveness. What arouses both of them partly is the way the other responds to spectacle: they watch each other's watching. This increases when they go to Pennyland, a kinetoscope arcade, to see the movies.[15]

The two films that they watch there are worth considering—again, not only because Algren uses them to prefigure the novel's later action but also because this scene opens up some interesting questions about spectatorship and identification in the novel. Before looking at them, however, I want to consider similar scenes in two novels that Algren admired: Stephen Crane's *Maggie: A Girl of the Streets* (1893) and Richard Wright's *Native Son* (1940).[16]

Maggie tells the story of two children of the New York Bowery, Maggie Johnson and her brother, Jimmie. Each is associated with one of the modes of street life: Jimmie with fighting and Maggie with daydreaming. Both are forms of performance. The modes of the street also have their professional equivalents. Street fighting professionalized is boxing; dreaming on the street graduates to "[losing] oneself" at the theater. Maggie is pursued by Pete, a former street fight champion; Pete takes her brother to "a boxing match in Williamsburg" and then takes Maggie to the theater.[17]

Crane's description of Pete's behavior toward Maggie in the theater and her response might have been a model for what Algren describes as happening between Bruno and Steffi at the amusement park. Maggie is mesmerized by the vaudeville acts: dancers, singers, comics, and minstrels. The ventriloquist presents "two fantastic dolls" that he makes "sing mournful ditties and say funny things about geography and Ireland."

"'Do dose little men talk?" asked Maggie. "Naw," said Pete, "it's some damn fake. See?'" (MGS, 32). Uninterested in the "fake," "Pete did not pay much attention to the progress of events upon the stage": "He was drinking beer and watching Maggie. Her cheeks were blushing with excitement and her eyes were glistening. She drew deep breaths of pleasure. No thoughts of atmosphere of the collar and cuff factory came to her" (MGS, 33).[18] Just as Bruno's interest lies less in the "fakery" of the amusements than in Steffi's excited breathing and what it might promise, so Pete is eager to leave the theater and straightforwardly demands "a kiss for takin' yeh teh deh show" (MGS, 33).

Crane is critical both of Maggie's inability to distinguish between the real and the "damn fake" and of Pete's blatant exploitation of that fact (it will end in her "ruin" and eventual death). After this first evening, Pete begins to take her regularly to the theater—most often to melodramas.

> Evenings during the week he took her to see plays in which the brain-clutching heroine was rescued from the palatial home of her guardian, who is cruelly after her bonds, by the hero with the beautiful sentiments. The latter spent most of his time out at soak in pale-green snow storms, busy with a nickel-plated revolver, rescuing aged strangers from villains.
>
> Maggie lost herself in sympathy with the wanderers swooning in snow storms beneath happy-hued church windows. And a choir within singing "Joy to the World." To Maggie and the rest of the audience this was transcendental realism. Joy always within, and they, like the actor, inevitably without. Viewing it, they hugged themselves in ecstatic pity of their imagined or real condition. (MGS, 32, 33, 37)

If Maggie's—and the rest of the audience's—easy response of "ecstatic pity" is not bad enough, Crane suggests, worse is the tendency of the melodramatic plot to make her "[lose] herself." The plays always suggest the inevitability of "a triumph for the hero, poor and of the masses, the representative of the masses, over the villain and the rich man." This, Crane wants to show, is not what really happens in the streets. There Maggie is seduced by Pete and in the eyes of the neighborhood—the same crowd that attends the theater—must now perform the role of fallen woman rather than heroine: "[S]he hung her head for she felt their eyes grimly upon her" (MGS, 74).

If the corruption of mass culture in the 1890s was epitomized by popular theater, by the 1940s the movies had taken over the role. The movie-watching scene in *Never Come Morning* might be read alongside its counterpart in *Native Son*, a work very much in Algren's mind when writing his own novel.[19] In Wright's novel, Bigger decides to take a job with the Daltons—and hence seals his fate—after seeing two movies: a "jungle movie" called *Trader Horn* (1930) and a rags-to-riches tale called *The Gay Woman* (n.d.).[20] As Bigger sits in the cinema, he translates his possible future life into a movie scenario; "Maybe Mr Dalton was a millionaire. Maybe he had a daughter who was a hot kind of girl; maybe she spent lots of money; maybe she'd like to come to the South Side and see the sights sometimes. Or maybe she would have a secret sweetheart and only he would know about it."[21] Throughout the novel, Bigger identifies with popular plots within which he can play no part. After he kills Mary, his first thought is that the situation is "unreal." His next is to remove his fingerprints because "he had read about them in magazines." After Mary's body is discovered in the furnace, he thinks qua Jimmy Cagney, "[H]e would shoot before he let them take him; it meant death either way, and he would die shooting every slug he had" (NS, 128–29; 260).[22]

For Wright and other Marxist critics of popular culture of the early 1940s, such identification is pernicious not only because it distracts the masses from the realities of their own lives but also because by doing so, it makes authentic choices and action impossible. At the end of the novel, Bigger's communist lawyer, Max Buckley, speaks in his defense to the judge, the jury, and, of course, the reader: "Your Honor, consider the mere physical aspect of our civilization. How alluring, how dazzling it is! How it excites the senses! How it seems to dangle within everyone the fulfillment of happiness! How constantly and overwhelmingly the advertisements, radios, newspapers, and movies play upon us! But in thinking of them remember that to many they are tokens of mockery. These bright colors may fill our hearts with elation, but to many they are daily taunts. Imagine a man walking amid such a scene, a part of it, and yet knowing that it is *not* for him! (NS, 429-30)

That this is also Wright's view is clear if we look at the comments with which he introduced his friend Algren's *Never Come Morning*. Wright's introduction expanded on the theme of what he termed "the tragically low quality of experience of the broad American masses": "Feverish radio programs, super advertisements, streamlined sky-scrapers, million-dollar movies, and mass production have somehow created the illusion in us that we are 'rich' in our emotional lives."[23]

As *Native Son* is, *Never Come Morning* is full of the stuff and promise of mass production, but Algren, I would suggest, is less dismissive of its value than Wright or Crane. At Riverview, Steffi confesses to Bruno that she loves "mov'n pictures, better'n anythin'" and her penny buys her a portion of *Blood and Sand* (1922), starring Rudolph Valentino and Nita Naldi.[24] Algren's choice of movie is hardly arbitrary, as *Blood and Sand* has many points of contact with *Never Come Morning*. Adapted by June Mathis from a novel by Vicente Blasco Ibáñez, it tells the story of a poor boy made both good and bad. Juan Gallardo (Valentino) kills a bull that has killed his friend and decides to become a bullfighter. He tells his mother (who is not dissimilar to Bruno's mother), "[S]omeday I'll build you a big house, and you'll have a fine carriage and all the silk dresses and shawls you want." Gallardo quickly becomes the idol of Seville, pursued by women wherever he goes. Initially, he is loyal to his childhood sweetheart, Carmen (Lita Lee), and they marry. After a particularly dramatic fight, however, he is seduced by an aristocratic vamp, Doña Sol (Naldi), who tells him, "Your muscles are like iron." He also meets a bandit, Plumitas, who is on the run from the police and who convinces him that they have a lot in common: both are poor boys who do violent things for money. Doña Sol runs off with Plumitas (in the erotic economy of violence, killing men is one step up from killing bulls), but the film ends with both men dead. First, Plumitas is gunned down by policemen lurking in the crowd at the corrida. Then Gallardo, who has lost his touch, is gored by the bull and dies, forming a beautiful pietà in his wife's arms. But the final words of the film are given to Gallardo's neighbor, Don Joselito (Charles Belcher), a "student of humanity" who provides a steady commentary on the action. Both bull and bullfighter, he says, are "beasts," but far worse is the fickle and sadistic crowd, "a beast with ten thousand heads." The presence of the student encourages us to read *Blood and Sand* as an allegory of Hollywood, and in particular, of its star system. "There was much in the character and experience of El Gallardo," says Valentino, "that I understood intimately and sympathetically."[25]

Although the film's story of out-of-the-ghetto sporting triumph might seem right up his street, Bruno is dismissive of Steffi's choice of film. "Lay off that old stuff," he tells her. "That guy was just a Dago when he was alive 'n he's only a coppy now" (NCM, 58). In the context of the novel as a whole, the words carry several layers of irony. First of all, Bruno's ready assertion of ethnic, tribal loyalty—that Valentino is not worth watching because he is "just a Dago"—will be central to both his boxing and his criminal careers (he fights "the Mexican" and kills "the Greek").[26] Second, he dismisses Valentino because he is "a coppy"—in other words, he is dead. But the phrase also evokes "copy": Valentino's image in the movie is simply one more "dummy" thing, and dummy things should be avoided.

In search of "live things," Bruno watches "a scarred and faded film of the Dempsey-Willard fight"—even older stuff, but an actual event and no mere fantasy (NCM, 57–58). Jack Dempsey fought Jess Willard for the heavyweight crown before "a shirt-sleeved frontier mob" in Toledo, Ohio, on the Fourth of July in 1919.[27] Willard entered the fight as the Great White Hope, who three years earlier had defeated Jack Johnson, the first black heavyweight champion. He was six feet seven inches tall and weighed in at two hundred and forty five pounds. Dempsey, six inches shorter and fifty-five pounds lighter, was definitely the underdog, needing, as Bruno says, "to prove himself."

Dempsey did indeed prove himself by defeating Willard with what boxing historians agree was an excess of violence.[28] In his

1950 teach-yourself guide to "explosive punching and aggressive defense," *Championship Fighting*, Dempsey recalled the fight:

> I sent Jess crashing to the canvas six or seven times in the first round and gave him such a battering in the third session that Jess was unable to come out for the fourth round. As Willard sat helplessly on his stool in the corner, his handlers threw in the towel just after the bell had rung to start the fourth. . . . I won the ring's most coveted title by stopping a man much larger and stronger than I was. . . . I blasted him into helplessness by exploding my body-weight against him. . . . My body-weight was moving like lightning, and I was exploding that weight terrifically against the giant. Even before the first round was finished, Willard looked like the victim of a premature mine blast.[29]

Although "Jack the Giant Killer" lost the championship in 1923 and finally retired in 1929, he remained an immensely popular figure during the Depression years. Horace Gregory's 1935 poem "Dempsey, Dempsey" is one of many that explored his appeal:

> When he's on his knees for a count
> And a million dollars cold,
> A million boys go down with him
> Yelling:
>   Hit him again Dempsey,
> Kill him for me Dempsey,
> . . . .
> Hit him again Dempsey, don't be a quitter
> Like I am Dempsey.[30]

Through Dempsey's victories, Gregory implies, "a million boys" feel themselves, momentarily at least, vindicated too. Turning "the film as slowly as possible," Bruno is one of those boys.[31]

> With his fighter's heart and his fighter's mind, Bruno sensed the mind and heart of the other. He watched Willard on his knees, swinging his head like a blinded ox, and no spark of pity came to the watcher. . . . His fingers spread, resisting the urge to get in there for the kill himself. He watched the ref standing Dempsey off, and that bothered both Dempsey and Bicek. He turned the film as slowly as possible. . . . Dempsey was circling, circling, trying to get at the beaten man on the other side of the referee's arm.

> A warmth rose in Bruno: Jack was in on the bum—one—two—left to the heart—right to the jaw—to the heart—to the jaw—and his hand stopped cold on the film. There was nothing before him but a cracked square of yellow cardboard and he was sweating on his hands. "We killed the bum fer life," he assured himself, "I'm a killer too." (NCM, 57–58)

Once again, Algren employs several levels of irony in this passage. In the novel's final fight, Bruno does metaphorically "kill" his opponent—Algren suggests this may partly be because it was "a white man's evening" (NCM, 260)—but he also literally kills "the Greek," and for that he is arrested as the final bell sounds. Algren also further explores the complexities of identifying with Dempsey. The identification is not primarily with his David-versus-Goliath-like success; it is with his anger, his ruthlessness, and his urge to "prove himself" at whatever cost: "No spark of pity came to the watcher," Algren writes. Identification here does not mean compassion; it means experience of another man's battles as your own. In order to do this Bruno turns the film "as slowly as possible"—adapting it, transforming it to suit his own needs. Earlier, he had needed Steffi's breathing to make him aware of his own excitement; here again, he needs another person's experience—Dempsey's circling as slowly as possible—as the medium through which to experience himself.

While Bigger Thomas is easily seduced by the plots of popular fiction, Wright (claiming a factual newspaper story as his source) never acknowledged their appeal to him. On the contrary. With *Never Come Morning,* Algren also began with a newspaper story, but the popular fictions that his characters enjoy, whether in movies or in sports, clearly also inform his work. I have suggested connections between *Blood and Sand* and Algren's novel; what about the Dempsey fight?

In his critical essays, Algren frequently drew an analogy between the writer and the fighter in order to discuss the nature of writing and the responsibilities and methods of the writer. This is *Nonconformity* again: "You don't write a novel out of sheer pity any more than you blow a safe out of vague longing to be rich. Compassion is all to the good, but vindictiveness is the verity Faulkner forgot: the organic force in every creative effort . . . that gives shape and color to all our dreams." The passage quickly moves onto an analogy with boxing, this time evoking Dempsey's 1921 opponent George Carpentier:

> "Vice, as vice, is bad and unwanted," the French light-heavyweight philosopher, Carpentier, once philosophized, "but there must be deep down in the makeup of every fighter a kind of viciousness."
>
> A certain ruthlessness and a sense of alienation from society is as essential to creative writing as it is armed robbery. The strong-armer isn't out merely to turn a fast buck any more than the poet is out solely to see his name on the cover of a book, whatever satisfaction that event may afford him. What both need most deeply is to get even.[32]

"Getting even" was something that connected the fighter and the writer—and something Algren particularly associated with Chicago, "the very toughest sort of town." "It used to be a writer's town and it's always been a fighter's town."[33] Bruno's ruthlessness and viciousness (his lack of pity) are qualities that Algren admires and perhaps shares; what distinguishes him from his character is a clear awareness that "getting even" with one's fists is no different from doing it in a movie or a novel: one is not more authentic than another; they are all performances.

Bruno does not take that fact into account when he distinguishes Valentino, the "coppy" actor, from Dempsey, the genuine fighter. But his firm distinction is further undermined if we consider the crossover between the respective careers of these two men. As soon as he became champion, Dempsey went to Hollywood in order to augment his earnings—highlights of his film career include the serials *Daredevil Jack* (1919) and *Fight and Win* (1922) as well as a 1933 feature, *The Prizefighter and the Lady*[34]—and to sleep with movie stars, including Mae West, Claudette Colbert, and Marion Davies. There, as Bruno does not seem to know, his friends included Douglas Fairbanks Sr., Charlie Chaplin, and Rudolph Valentino. In 1925, Valentino trained with Dempsey—and Gene Lamont—for his 1925 film, *Cobra*. Valentino's character answers a rival's charge that he is an "indoor sheikh" with a knockout punch. This was sadly to prove another self-reflexive Hollywood moment. The following year Valentino's death, at thirty-one, was hastened by boxing injuries. Suffering from acute peritonitis, he nevertheless staged a bout to challenge a *Chicago Tribune* journalist who, in the famous "Pink Powder Puff" attack, questioned his manhood and called him a Dago.[35] "I defy you," replied Valentino, "to meet me in the boxing . . . arena to prove in typical American fashion . . . which of us is more a man."[36] As does Bruno, all that Valentino wanted, wrote John Dos Passos in *The Big Money* (1936), was " to make good in he-man, two-fisted, . . . America."[37]

Although he makes a firm distinction between Dempsey and Valentino, Bruno often finds it hard to distinguish real boxers from actors playing boxers in his daydream. The scene I have been discussing is not the only one in which Algren describes Bruno's mind as "swamped" with images of himself in the ring and not the only time Bruno adjusts the speed of the projection in order to create his own movie. During his fight with Pinsky—"the Jew who had taken the title off Tiger Pultoric on a fluke, after Pultoric had beaten Louis on points"—Bruno's mind feels "as though he had been abruptly transplanted before a technicolor movie being reeled a little too fast" (NCM, 89). Pinsky has bags under his eyes, "like that John Barrymore in the movies had," he notes, and Bruno himself rubs his jaw "reflectively, the way he'd seen Jimmy Cagney do it" (NCM, 89–91).[38] The movies infect every aspect of Bruno's, as well as Steffi's, life, even Bruno's time in the ring, the time when, he tells her, "I don't feel like no dummy" (NCM, 54).

For Wright, violence is the opposite of fakery—a guarantor of authenticity. Max, who seems to have read Jean-Paul Sartre more recently than Karl Marx, explains to the court that while the murder of Mary Dalton was nothing more than an accident, Bigger's acceptance of the crime "was the first full act of his life": "He accepted it because it made him free, gave him the possibility of choice, of action, the opportunity to act and to feel that his actions carried weight." Bigger echoes, "I didn't know I was really alive in this world until I felt things hard enough to kill for 'em" (NS, 430). As we have seen, Bruno makes the same kind of claim: that when scrappin', he feels no dummy. By writing about boxing rather than murder, Algren, however, highlighted the performance in the violence. Bigger commits his murder alone, with the author his only spectator.[39] But Bruno is not alone; his act of violence takes place in front of a crowd and under artificial lights. The novel begins and ends with the sound of the bell; the action within it has been as contained as that of a boxing match itself.[40] There is no outside, no superior perspective; no lawyer or "student of humanity" interpreting things for us.

As Wright does, Algren often portrays popular culture as something that provides its consumers with both escape (from one's own self) and imprisonment (by imaginary selves). For example, we hear that the women in the brothel are restless when the jukebox and slot machine are switched off, for "Silence, like daylight, brought them all back into themselves" (NCM, 167). But coming back to oneself is something that no one, it seems, can stand for very long.[41]

In *Hard Facts: Setting and Form in the American Novel*, Philip Fisher discusses the rise and fall of the Ferris wheel and the rocking chair as symbols of naturalist structure in Theodore Dreiser's *Sister Carrie* (1900). Launched at the 1893 Chicago Exposition, the Ferris wheel was, he points out, particularly associated with "that city's coming of age" and a powerful symbol of "the tragical and vertical motions of rising and falling," "canceling the effects of motion by allowing it to recur in the same place."[42] At the amusement park, Steffi persuades Bruno to take her not on the Ferris wheel but on the roller coaster. While both the Ferris wheel and the rocking chair suggest the futile energies of the naturalist movement, Algren's roller coaster, I would suggest, more vividly evokes the naturalist arc of slow rise and rapid decline. It also provides us with another moment of spectatorship.

At the top, Steffi buries her head against Bruno, "fearing to look" down, but Bruno "forced himself to look": "[T]housands of little people and hundreds of bright little stands, and over it all the coal-smoke pall of the river factories and railroad yards. He saw *in that moment* the whole dim-lit city on the last night of summer; the troubled streets that led to the abandoned beaches, the for-rent signs above overnight hotels and furnished basement rooms, moving trolleys and rising bridges: the cagework city, between a coal-smoke sky" (NCM, 61–62; my emphasis). Above the city, just "in that moment," Bruno assumes a detached sociological perspective on the city and on his life. (Carla Cappetti finds an echo of

Robert E. Park's "mosaic city" in Bruno's "cagework city.")[43] But that potentially liberating perspective can only, Algren insists, be momentary. As the car begins to descend not steadily but "div[ing] as though shoved off a roof," Bruno too descends into the personal, experiencing, first, disillusionment ("'The park's a fake,' the boy thought hurriedly") and then rage ("the hell with everything") (NCM, 62). It is at this point that he decides to get Steffi drunk, with a beer bearing the legend of Tiger Pultoric (the escapism of drink and of sporting dreams in one bottle). He then takes her to the warehouse, where the gang soon arrives, demanding "a shot" at her. As the gang rape proceeds, the amusement park imagery returns. As the boys push each other out of the way, saying, "It ain't no peep show," Bruno goes in search of drink: "There was a great wheel beginning to turn, slowly and heavily, in his stomach, and he had to have liquor to make it go faster and faster, till he was blind with its turning; till its turning was a blindness in his mind for a month" (NCM, 70). This is perhaps as far from the sociological detachment of the bird's-eye view as one can get. Bruno's understanding of the city's workings is now fully internalized, fully visceral.

Steffi also has a moment of sociological clarity. In a key scene near the novel's end, we are told that she suddenly "saw Bruno clearly" and "without love." In that moment, he is merely "a duped hoodlum who had kicked her into the gutter and let her lie because others might laugh if he helped her up." Steffi too has adopted the impersonal objective perspective of the naturalist observer, but once again she can sustain it, Algren adds, "only for a moment" (NCM, 246). Both Bruno and Steffi quickly fall back into rage and disgust, love and pity—the sentiments that, I have suggested, also motivate Algren's writing.

In his classic exposition of naturalist technique, Émile Zola compared writing a novel to performing a laboratory experiment—an experiment in which the effects of a specific heredity and environment on a character or group of characters were to be observed. For the experiment to be successful, however, it had to be performed in a carefully controlled environment, with the "experimenter" following what he termed the "impersonal" method. The whole point of naturalist observation was to move away from "personal fantasy."[44]

Algren certainly located himself in what had by 1942 become a well-established "experimental" tradition. As we have seen, Algren claimed that *Never Come Morning* was "a thinly fictionalized report on a neighborhood" and that it tested the thesis that environment determines the fates of those unable to leave its "ring of fire."[45] But to test such a thesis the ring must be clearly seen and mapped, and this can be done only from above. What I have been suggesting here is how fleetingly Algren, as the roller-coaster car does, lingers at the top of the rise.

Five years after *Never Come Morning* was published, Malcolm Cowley published "Not Men: A Natural History of American Naturalism," in which he complained of the "superior and ultimately tiresome" attitude of writers such as Frank Norris and Dreiser. "Irony—like pity, its companion—is a spectator's emotion, and it sets a space between ourselves and the characters in the novel. They suffer, but their cries reach us faintly, like those of dying strangers we cannot hope to save."[46] Cowley's terms seem very different from Zola's. He speaks of irony, pity, and compassion; Zola, of "the impersonal." Both, however, adopt a model of spectatorship that depends on distance and superiority—to return to Whitman the sociologist again, a model that means speaking *for* your characters. Algren's narrative spectatorship is sometimes "ironic" and even occasionally impersonal but these are positions his writing struggles to maintain. More generally, Algren presents the activity of looking as the opposite of detached. Identification (being *of* rather than speaking *for*) is inevitable, as is the intrusion of what Zola called "personal fantasy." (If the uneducated Bruno compared himself to Cagney and Dempsey, the highly educated Simone de Beauvoir compared Algren to Edward G. Robinson.)[47] As his characters, Algren was unable to look very long without love—which prompted him to "make it up" to his characters—or without hate, which prompted him to "get even" on their behalf. Love and hate are complementary impulses for him. In a preface to a 1962 anthology, Algren compared what he calls Bigger Thomas's "creative act" of murder with the impetus behind Joseph Conrad's fiction: "That his [Conrad's] was an act of love while Bigger Thomas's was an act of hate is irrelevant: whenever you shut a human being out of the world, he will, for better or for worse, build one of his own."[48]

Notes

1. Those who argue against thinking of Algren as a naturalist include George Bluestone, "Nelson Algren," *Western Review* 22 (1957) 27–44, and R. W. Lid, "A World Imagined,"176–96, in *American Literary Naturalism: A Reassessment*, ed. Yoshinobu Hakutani and Lewis Fried (Heidelberg, Germany: Carl Winter Universitätsverlag, 1975). James R. Giles argues that Algren "re-invents naturalism." *Confronting the Horror: The Novels of Nelson Algren* (Kent, Ohio: Kent State University Press, 1989), 4. Carla Cappetti suggests that "naturalism" has become an unhelpful "catch-all term. It reveals little about so-called naturalist writers and texts but a great deal about . . . post–WWII American literary criticism . . . to use the label *naturalism* is either to be patronizing or dismissive." Nevertheless, she does not wish to discard the term. *Writing Chicago: Modernism, Ethnography and the Novel* (New York: Columbia University Press, 1993), 3.

2. Nelson Algren, quoted in *Writers at Work: The Paris Review Interviews*, First Series (1955), ed. Malcolm Cowley (Harmondsworth, England: Penguin, 1977), 238.

3. Ibid., 241.

4. Ibid., 245.

5. *Never Come Morning* (1942; repr., New York: Seven Stories Press, 1996), 8. Further references are to this edition and are cited parenthetically as NCM.

6. Walt Whitman, "You Felons on Trial in Courts," no. 13 in *Leaves of Grass* (1860), and under this title in the 1867 edition. Quoted in *Leaves of Grass: Inclusive Edition*, ed. Emory Holloway (New York: Doubleday, Doran, 1927), 323.

7. The Polish daily paper *Zgoda* had written "in his treatment of inmates of houses of ill repute he is in an element all his own and no doubt was on a narcotic jag when he concocted this story" (NCM, preface, xi). Bettina Drew discusses the Sawicki trial as a source for the novel, in *Nelson Algren: A Life on the Wild Side* (London: Bloomsbury, 1990), 134–35.

8. Rolf Lindner, *The Reportage of Urban Culture: Robert Park and the Chicago School*, trans. Adrian Morris (Cambridge: Cambridge University Press, 1996), 172. Lindner emphasizes Park's roots in journalism, including his involvement with the College of Journalism, where Algren studied sociology. On Park's interest in Whitman, see also Cappetti, *Writing Chicago*, 24–25.

9. Preface to *Leaves of Grass* (1855), in *The Portable Walt Whitman*, ed. Mark Van Doren (Harmondsworth, England: Penguin, 1945), 15.

10. On the relationship between what she calls Whitman's "chant of equivalence" and his syntax, see Wai Chee Dimock, "Whitman, Syntax, and Political Theory," 62–79, in *Breaking Bounds: Whitman and American Cultural Studies*, ed. Betsy Erkkila and Jay Grossman (Oxford: Oxford University Press, 1996), 78. See also David Simpson, "Destiny Made Manifest: The Styles of Whitman's Poetry," in *Nation and Narration*, ed. Homi K. Bhabha (London: Routledge, 1990), 177–96.

11. Quoted in *Leaves of Grass* (New York: 1855), 29, 53, 56.

12. Algren, quoted in Drew, *Nelson Algren*, 112.

13. F. Scott Fitzgerald, quoted in Nelson Algren, *Nonconformity: Writing on Writing* (New York: Seven Stories Books, 1996), 28.

14. Bluestone, *Nelson Algren*, 31.

15. Laura Rabinovitz discusses "cinema at the amusement park" at the turn of the century, with particular reference to and with illustrations of Riverview. *For the Love of Pleasure: Women, Movies and Culture in Turn-of-the Century Chicago* (New Brunswick, N.J.: Rutgers University Press, 1998), ch. 5.

16. When asked by the *Paris Review* about influences, Algren replied, "Well, I used to like Stephen Crane a lot" *Writers at Work*, 240.

17. Stephen Crane, *Maggie: A Girl of the Streets* (1893; repr., Harmondsworth, England: Penguin, 2000), 37, 23. Further references are to this edition and are cited parenthetically as MGS. See Thomas A. Gullason, "Tragedy and Melodrama in Stephen Crane's *Maggie*," in *Maggie: A Girl of the Streets* (New York: Norton, 1979), 245–53.

18. Compare this passage with Jane Addams's account of "going to the show" in her investigative study *The Spirit of Youth and the City Streets*: "The theater is the only place where [young people] can satisfy the craving for a conception of life higher than that which the world actually offers them. . . . The theater becomes to them a 'veritable house of dreams' infinitely more real than the noisy streets and crowded factories. . . . And yet the whole apparatus for supplying pleasure is wretchedly inadequate and full of danger to whomsoever may approach it" (New York: Macmillan, 1909), 75–76, 15.

19. Wright too had taken a series of newspaper stories as the starting point for his novel; in his case, it was the *Chicago Tribune*'s coverage of the trial of Robert Nixon, a young black man who had confessed to killing five women and raping others. See Margaret Walker, *Richard Wright: Daemonic Genius* (New York: Amistad, 1988), 122–25. Wright's model in turn was, he told Walker, Dreiser's *American Tragedy* (1925). Algren told Wright that *Native Son* had "slugged him out of a coma." Quoted in Drew, *Nelson Algren*, 125.

20. Irving Thalberg's African trader adventure *Trader Horn* (1930) was described by *Variety* magazine as a "sure money-getter": "Outstanding animal stuff, great sound effects, and thin story, which has good-looking white girl romping around scantily clad." Quoted in *Halliwell's Film and Video Guide*, 12th ed., ed. John Walker (London: HarperCollins, 1997), 771. Although gay brides, brothers, desperadoes, diplomats, divorcees, duelists, imposters, intruders, old dogs, shoe clerks, and sisters all exist on celluloid, I can find no mention of *The Gay Woman*.

21. Richard Wright, *Native Son* (1940; repr., Harmondsworth, England: Penguin, 1972), 72–73. Further references are to this edition and are cited parenthetically as NS.

22. See Ross Pudaloff, "Celebrity as Identity: *Native Son* and Mass Culture," in *Richard Wright: Critical Perspectives Past and Present*, ed. Henry Louis Gates Jr. and K. A. Appiah (New York: Amistad, 1993), 156–70.

23. Richard Wright, introduction to *Never Come Morning* (New York: Harper & Row, 1942), quoted in Drew, *Nelson Algren*, 141. In the essay "Community Organization and Juvenile Delinquency," 99–112, Robert E. Park ar-

gued that mass culture (particularly "[t]he newspaper and the motion picture show") can lead to what, quoting Alfred Adler, he refers to as "psychic overcompensation," a state that includes a "penchant for the fantastic, . . . [an] estrangement from reality." He also seeks support from Whitman's lines praising animals: "No one is dissatisfied—not one is demented with the mania of owning / things." Robert E. Park, Ernest W. Burgess, and Roderick D. McKenzie, *The City* (1925; repr., Chicago: University of Chicago Press, 1967), 102, 108.

24. *Blood and Sand* was directed by Fred Niblo. Later in the novel, Steffi remembers that when she was a child, "she had loved to skate to the library and look at the books with the brightest pictures, and skate back carrying the pictures in her mind," 252.

25. Quoted in Theodore Huff, "The Career of Rudolph Valentino," *Films in Review*, 146, and Emily W. Leider, *Dark Lover: The Life and Death of Rudolph Valentino* (London: Faber, 2003), 204. See also David Bret, *Valentino* (London: Robson Books, 1998), 75–81.

26. See Ian Peddie, "Poles Apart? Ethnicity, Race, Class, and Nelson Algren," *Modern Fiction Studies* 47, no. 1 (Spring 2001): 118–44.

27. Thomas Healey, *A Hurting Business* (London: Picador, 1996), 17.

28. Peter Heller describes the fight as "one of the most savage in boxing history." *"In This Corner . . . !"* (London: Rolson Books, 1973), 55.

29. Jack Dempsey, *Championship Fighting*, ed. Jack Cuddy (London: Nicholas Kaye, 1950), 8–9.

30. Horace Gregory, "Dempsey, Dempsey," in *Proletarian Literature in the United States: An Anthology*, ed. Granville Hicks et al. (London: Martin Lawrence, 1935), 161–62.

31. Thomas Healey is another. His 1996 memoir *A Hurting Business* is structured as a fight in fifteen rounds. In the first round/chapter, his father is beaten in a carnival booth as he had been by the school tough girl, Brenda Kane. Soon afterward, he sees the film of Jack Dempsey beating Jess Willard—"he was the best at violence I'd seen"—and later that evening, loses his virginity to Brenda—"*what* a night," he recalls, "Brenda and Jack Dempsey," 25. For more on Healey, see Kasia Boddy, "Scottish Fighting Men: Big and Wee," in *Scotland in Theory*, ed. Eleanor Bell and Gavin Miller (Amsterdam: Rodopi, 2004), 183–96.

32. *Nonconformity*, 33–34. Jack Dempsey beat the French boxer Georges Carpentier in "boxing's first million-dollar gate," on July 2, 1921. Harry Mullan, *The Illustrated History of Boxing* (London: Hamlyn, 1990), 32. The fight forms the basis of Ring Lardner's story "The Battle of the Century" (1921). When asked by H. E. F. Donohue whether he was a violent person, Algren answered: "No, I don't react very quickly. I've known men who do spontaneously know whether to knock somebody cold. But I'm afraid I have to go home and think about it for three days and decide it was justified and say now if you would stand exactly in the same position you were when you said that, now I'm going to give it to you, see. But the occasion is gone. This can leave a little rankling." *Conversations with Nelson Algren* (New York: Hill & Wang, 1964), 77–78. Hemingway's cover blurb for Algren's first novel stated, "You should not read *Somebody in Boots* if you cannot take a punch."

33. Nelson Algren, *Chicago: City on the Make* (Garden City, N.Y.: Doubleday, 1951), 69. In several other places, Algren considers the notion that successful fighters must have the need either to "prove" themselves or to "get even." In a story called "Depend on Aunt Elly," for example, Baby Needles is simply a "ring clown": "You couldn't make him mad." His great moment occurs when his girlfriend, Wilma, finally does make him mad. "The great strength of a fighting man is his pride," says a character in another story; the only problem is, as yet another points out, "when you're thirty-two and have been at this trade thirteen years, you've pretty well used up your hostility." "He Swung and He Missed," in *The Neon Wilderness* (1947; repr., New York: Hill & Wang, 1960), 161; "Dark Came Early in That Country," in *The Last Carousel* (New York: G. Putnam's, 1973), 3.

34. Bret, *Valentino*, 32; 151–52. See also Roger Kahn, *A Flame of Pure Fire: Jack Dempsey and the Roaring '20s* (San Diego: Harvest Books, 1999).

35. What became known as the "Pink Powder Puff" attack was published in the *Chicago Tribune* on July 18, 1926. Valentino's interest in boxing was due partly to a need to prove himself properly masculine in the American grain. The tango was not enough. "While we try to assure ourselves in this country," wrote Veras Caspary in 1926, "that dancing is as masculine as boxing and the dancer the physical peer of the fighter, we don't honestly believe it." "The Twilight of the Dance Gods: Merely a Theory Regarding Masculine Arms and Feminine Ankles," *The Dance* 6, no. 2 (1926); 19. Quoted in Gaylyn Studlar, *This Mad Masquerade: Stardom and Masculinity in the Jazz Age* (New York: Columbia University Press, 1996), 185. See also Miriam Hansen, *Babel and Babylon: Spectatorship in American Silent Film* (Cambridge, Mass.: Harvard University Press, 1991).

36. Leider, *Dark Lover*, 374.

37. John Dos Passos, *The Big Money*, in *U.S.A.* (1936; repr., London: John Lehman, 1950), 841.

38. *Never Come Morning* is set during the Depression of the 1930s, a period dominated by escapist films of all kinds. One popular genre was that of the "boxer-made-good," two of which featured Cagney himself: *The Irish in Us* (1935) and *City for Conquest* (1940). Robert Sklar argues that Cagney "established a new cultural type on the American screen and in the world's imagination. It was the urban tough guy—small, wiry, savvy, and street-smart—a figure out of the immigrant ghettoes and ethnic neighborhoods of Chicago and New York." *City Boys: Cagney, Bogart, Garfield* (Princeton, N.J.: Princeton University Press, 1992), 12. Dempsey's appeal seems similar. The "Jack Dempsey of the small men," the '30s Glasgow flyweight champion Benny Lynch was also compared to Cagney. "'Christ Benny, you were Jimmy Cagney in *White Heat* there the night," said one of the seconds'" after he won in 1934. John Burrowes, *Benny: The Life and Times of a Fighting* Legend (Edinburgh, Scotland: Mainstream, 1982), 199, 151. While films of the early 1930s (such as *The Public Enemy*) tended to suggest that crime was a viable route to individual success, by the end of the decade, it was portrayed as the regretful product of poor environments. One of Algren's sources may have been a long-running series of films about a gang variously known as the Dead End Kids, the East End Kids, and the

Bowery Boys, films that emphasized the sociology behind the gangster myth and thus tried to undermine its glamour. The gang first appeared in Sidney Kingsley's 1937 hit play, *Dead End,* and then in the film version, written by Lillian Hellman and directed by William Wyler. Approximately eighty-five films were made, featuring either the Dead End Kids or Bowery Boys. *They Made Me a Criminal* (1939), for example, features the Dead End kids alongside John Garfield as a prizefighter framed for a murder. See David Hayes and Brent Walker, *The Films of the Bowery Boys* (New York: Citadel Press, 1984). It was not, however, until the 1940s that the boxing movie, like *Never Come Morning,* became infused with the pessimism and masochism of noir. Another popular series featured the "fallen woman." See Andrew Bergman, *We're in the Money: Depression America and Its Films* (Chicago: Ivan R. Dee, 1971), especially chapters 4 and 11. *Never Come Morning* could fruitfully be read in relation to movies of both these genres.

39. Quoting Bigger's statement "what I killed for, I am," Harold Kaplan argues for the redemptive quality of violence in naturalist fiction. *Power and Order: Henry Adams and the Naturalist Tradition in American Fiction* (Chicago: University of Chicago Press, 1981), ch. 6. Reading the same passage, Pudaloff, however, points out that "the sincerity of this statement not withstanding, it fails to distinguish an authentic personal identity from an identity framed by mass culture." In other words, at this final moment, Bigger is still playing the Cagneyesque "tough guy," 164.

40. Brecht presented plays such as *In the Jungle of Cities* (1924) as boxing matches in order to challenge the audience's emotional involvement; behaving as a boxing crowd, he maintained, would make the theater audience more objective. Algren, on the other hand, did not find objectivity in the fight crowd, only theatrical involvement. See Franco Ruffini, "A Little More Healthy Sport! Bertolt Brecht and Objective Boxing," *Mime Journal* (1996): 2–15. Cappetti argues that Algren's use of the city is "Brechtian-like," *Writing Chicago,* 175.

41. Talking elsewhere about his love of theater, Algren admitted his attraction lay in "the whole idea of make-believe": "I believe most people who fool around with fiction . . . believe there's only one real world and that's the make-believe world, the world that Tennessee Williams created in *Streetcar Named Desire,* a world a lot more real than the real world. I think the important thing is the make-believe world." Quoted in Donohue, *Conversations with Nelson Algren,* 97.

42. Philip Fisher, *Hard Facts: Setting and Form in the American Novel* (Oxford, England: Oxford University Press, 1987), 154.

43. Cappetti, *Writing Chicago,* 173–74.

44. Émile Zola, "The Experimental Novel" (1880), 162–96, in *Documents of Modern Literary Realism,* ed. George J. Becker (Princeton, N.J.: Princeton University Press, 1963), 188–89.

45. Algren claimed that his aim was to describe "the *routine lives* of people just *living* in that kind of ring of fire to show how you can't get out of a certain neighborhood." *Writers at Work,* 245. Algren concedes to Donohue that his "form of reportage" might be called "emotionalized reportage," 154.

46. Malcolm Cowley, "Not Men: A Natural History of American Naturalism" (1947), 429–51, in *Documents of Modern Literary Realism*, 450.

47. In 1957 de Beauvoir dedicated her novel *The Mandarins* to Algren, who appears in it thinly disguised as Lewis Brogan. "At first, I had found it amusing meeting in the flesh that classic American species: self-made leftist writer. Now, I began taking an interest in Brogan. Through his stories, you got the feeling that he claimed no rights on life and that nevertheless he had always had a passionate desire to live. I liked that mixture of modesty and eagerness. . . . He was speaking rapidly and I had a little trouble following him, but I found it as exciting as an Edward G. Robinson film." Trans. Leonard M. Friedman (Glasgow: Fontana, 1982), 407.

48. Nelson Algren, preface to *Nelson Algren's Book of Lonesome Monsters* (1962; repr., London: Panther, 1964), 7.

Making Nakedness Visible: Narrative Perspective in Nelson Algren's *The Man with the Golden Arm*

James R. Giles

In a 1998 study Christophe Den Tandt argues that there are two distinct kinds of response to the "foreignness" and sheer incomprehensibleness of the American city in texts by turn-of-the-century American literary naturalists. In Den Tandt's view, Theodore Dreiser, especially in *Sister Carrie* (1900), responds in an affirmative way to the impossibility of perceiving the full complexity of the newly emerging American city. Consequently, Dreiser turns to the natural world to discover metaphors for the "magic," the "radically novel form of enchantment" embodied in such a diverse and constantly changing space. Den Tandt defines this response as the "oceanic sublime."[1] In contrast, Frank Norris and Jack London, when describing the city, write out of a negative perspective that Den Tandt labels the "naturalist gothic": "[T]he sublime features of the gothic genre are grounded in effects of depth and intensity; they are rooted in a fascination with physical deformity, horror, and hidden recesses of experience. Rhetorically, the discourse of the grotesque—with its allusions to the 'fearful slime,' the 'twisted monstrosities,' or the 'creatures of prey' of the urban crowd—is sublime because it systematically relies on hyperbole."[2]

In texts by Norris, London, and other turn-of-the-century "naturalist gothic" writers, slums become foreign spaces inhabited by "twisted monstrosities," by "creatures of prey." The relative narrowness of such urban spaces expedites external surveillance and control. Michel Foucault's adaptation of Jeremy Bentham's Panopticon is applicable here. Norris's grotesque denizens of San Francisco in *McTeague* (1899) and the strange beings that London discovers dwelling in the East End of London are observed, controlled, and punished by capitalist society and by the novelists who envision them. For Norris—the product of an upper-middle class background—the denizens of Polk Street are foreign and threatening. Consequently, McTeague, Trina, Maria Macapa, Marcus, and Zerkow are all condemned to a horrible death. Jack London's impoverished residents of England's capital city are isolated and objectified by the very costume of their poverty—in contrast to the narrator, who can move in and out of the East End simply by changing clothing and who describes them as a "new and different race" of gorillalike creatures.[3]

Den Tandt's argument evolves from June Howard's analysis of the common narrative perspective of naturalism in which "privileged readers" are gathered together "to stare anxiously at the specter of proletarianization."[4] Traditional literary naturalism privileges narrative distance, perspectives from outside and above characters, perspectives that further objectify socioeconomic victims. Nelson Algren revolutionized American literary naturalism by deliberately undercutting that privileged narrative perspective. Moreover, he challenged it through a complex aesthetic that initially seems to reproduce it. That aesthetic can be illustrated through five memorable instances of narrative perspective from *The Man with the Golden Arm* (1949), a text that is, on the surface, a particularly grotesque example of Den Tandt's "naturalist gothic."

The first of these instances occurs in the novel's opening scene, in which the protagonist, Frankie Machine, and his companion, Sparrow Saltskin, have been arrested and, after being questioned by Record Head Bednar, are locked inside a jail cell.[5] The two can anticipate their sentences before hearing them since arrest and incarceration have become preordained, indeed scripted, occasions in their lives and thus have more to do with what they are than with anything they have done. In this scene, Algren indirectly emphasizes his variation of naturalistic determinism by having Frankie, Sparrow, and Bednar perform as if they are repeating roles in a very long-running play, a play that has in fact become their lives. They exchange absurdist dialogue that each knows by heart and with which each is, in fact, more than a little bored:

[Bednar]:	What kind of [military] discharge you get, Dealer?
[Frankie]:	The *right* kind. *And* the Purple Heart.
[Bednar]:	Who do you fight with?
[Frankie]:	My wife, that's all.
[Bednar]:	Hell, that's no crime.[6]

Sparrow emphasizes the matter-of-fact nature of the incident when he tells Bednar: "After all, everybody got to get arrested now 'n then, I'm no better'n anybody else. . . . I'm unincapable, that's all" (MGA, 6). Frankie understands the real reason for their arrest: it serves as a notice to Zero Schwiefka, the petty criminal for whom Frankie deals poker, that Zero is a week behind in making payoffs to the police. In a sense, all of the characters in Algren's text, including Record Head Bednar, are Zeros since none of them is in control of his life. Control, the text asserts here, lies in a realm of the Chicago bureaucratic-police hierarchy so vague and so remote that it cannot even be envisioned. Still it cannot be resisted:

> That was the way things were because that was how things had always been. Which was why they could never be any different. Neither God, war, nor the ward super work any deep change on West Division Street.
>
> For here God and the ward super work hand in hand and neither moves without the other's assent. God loans the super cunning and the super forwards a percentage of the grift on Sunday mornings. The super puts in the fix for all right-thinking hustlers and the Lord, in turn, puts in the fix for the super. For the super's God is a hustler's God; and as wise, in his way, as the God of the priests and the businessmen. (MGA, 9)

Algren has elevated the privileged reader, presumably a middle-class one, to an Olympian perspective. In this opening scene, the narrative perspective provides the reader with a detached view of the foreign world of petty crime and police surveillance in the city. It also provides reassurance that this world is so determined that no aspect of it, including the graft, can or even should be altered. After all, Frankie and the Sparrow do end up in jail, where they should be because it is where they so often have been. Most importantly, the scene *seems* to establish a fundamental difference in kind between the middle-class reader and such amusingly grotesque characters as Frankie and the Sparrow. In fact, the emphasis on the comic absurdity of their lives appears to constitute an additional dimension in the process of their dehumanization. They thus seem amusing—and consequently, nonthreatening—residents of a no longer "fearful" urban "slime." The very prison setting of this opening scene reassures the "respectable" middle-class reader. Even though they are hardly frightening, Frankie and Sparrow are, at the very heart of their being, somehow illegal and thus need to be confined.

The narrative logic of the scene is intensely voyeuristic—a perspective that Den Tandt argues is common in the "naturalist gothic." The safely removed reader can view Frankie and Sparrow in a prison, an unnatural space functioning as a synecdoche for the ghetto itself, itself an unnatural space that is contained through a process of constant surveillance and arbitrary punishment. After all, everybody the Sparrow knows gets arrested "now 'n then."

A different kind of voyeurism is apparent in the second instance of narrative perspective. Near the end of the novel, Molly Novotny, the habitually victimized woman who loved Frankie Machine, has taken a job as a stripper in a black nightclub. It would seem difficult to imagine a more inherently voyeuristic act than a striptease, the very dynamic of which works through the commodification and objectification of naked or seminaked female bodies that are, for a price, exhibited to an anonymous audience to observe and observe only. The eroticism of the striptease is based then on a distance, on lack of contact. Algren implicitly makes the reader part of the audience observing Molly-O and the rest of a "chorus": "A brown and white chorus came out one by one, seemingly too indifferent toward each other to come out together, till there were five. Though each wore only slippers and a G-string, all seemed overdressed, so studiously had their nakedness been donned. Each pore powdered, each taut pink nipple tinted with fingernail polish and dusted with some mauve talc, the armpits shaven and deodorized, each navel dusted and the hair swept back behind each small catlike ear" (MGA, 302–3).

In his informative 1963 work of nonfiction *Who Lost an American?* Algren attacks the "third-person morality" of Hugh Hefner, the personification of a new Chicago. Hefner and the 1950s urban American male to whom his Playboy empire were dedicated are, Algren asserts, reincarnations of the male American Puritan of the eighteenth century who hated women for possessing a body that evoked in him sexual responses of which he was ashamed. A comparable assumption underlies the scene. Men pay to observe the virtually nude Molly-O and her companions, who are forced to enter one at a time isolated and vulnerable. Still, the men are allowed to view not a real, but an artificial, a costumed, nudity. Genuine nakedness would evoke not simply a sexual response in the audience but also an awareness of the essential humanness of the five women. Such an awareness would threaten to destroy the safe distance established between the men and the women they have gone there to observe.

Den Tandt argues that the "naturalist gothic" depends on "a discourse of gendered economics expressing itself allegorically, through a display of libidinal monsters."[7] The kind of striptease described by Algren makes literal a gendered economics. In it the female-body-as-commodity is displayed directly and without a protective layer of metaphor. Costumed nudity, but not authentic human nakedness, is described in sufficient detail that the voyeuristic reader can observe "pink nipples," "navels," and carefully shaven "armpits." The voyeuristic reader has, in effect, been Hefnerized in this passage. The carefully sanitized and dehumanized nature of the monthly pinups in *Playboy* has been repeatedly and convincingly analyzed.

Yet throughout the novel the privileged position of the reader as voyeur is undercut by the text's depiction of Molly-O as a brave young woman whose humanness has not been fundamentally compromised by the relentless victimization that constitutes her life. Molly-O is no "libidinal monster." In fact, the underlying aesthetic of *The Man with the Golden Arm* rests in affirmation of the inherent humanness not only of Molly-O but even of the deliberately filthy and undeniably grotesque Blind Pig, who chronically smiles at his mental image of a burlesque runaway and thus seems very much a "libidinal monster."

For the third instance of narrative perspective, we return to the opening prison scene, in which Frankie Machine, in a passage that has been analyzed often, himself assumes a voyeuristic position in order to observe a cockroach struggling to escape from a water bucket outside his cell. Frankie's observation of the endangered insect begins as a means of passing time and fighting boredom in his prison cell. He promises himself that upon release from the cell, he will save the roach. But not untypically, he forgets and the roach drowns, and Frankie suddenly becomes a sophisticated interpreter of symbolic incident: "It was too late all right. Too late for roaches or old Skid Row rumdums; it was even getting a little late for cripples and junkies and punks too long on the same old hustle. The water-soaked corpse was only half afloat, the head submerged and the rear end pointing to the ceiling like a sinking sub when the perpetual waters pull it downward and down forever. 'I could have saved him,' Frankie realized with a faint remorse. 'It's all my fault again' " (MGA, 27).

Frankie's narrative perspective undergoes a significant shift in this scene. Initially, he is comparable to the implied middle-class reader in the opening-scene passage describing the imperceptible but no less inescapable bureaucratic-police power. Frankie observes the drowning roach with a detachment comparable to the reader when witnessing the dealer's incarceration. For Frankie, the insect's plight is as boring as Bednar's questioning of Sparrow and him: boring and *threatening*. Frankie makes a metaphoric connection first between the roach and "old Skid Row rumdums." Since he is not himself an alcoholic, that initial application of the metaphor is not personally threatening to Frankie, but the rest of it decidedly is. He is addicted to morphine, is in fact a "junkie," and has been arrested precisely because he has been "too long on the same old hustle."

As I have argued elsewhere, the "remorse" that suddenly assaults Frankie over his failure to save the roach and that causes him to "confess," "It's all my fault again" is clearly applicable to the guilt that has always haunted Frankie and has resulted in his inability to care for himself or anyone else. In this scene Algren turns to literary existentialism to convey Frankie's unfeelingness.

As Roquentin is in Jean-Paul Sartre's *Nausea* (1938), Frankie is at once terrified of, and bored by, the sheer facticity in which he is trapped.[8]

Paradoxically, that seemingly sourceless guilt that denies Frankie the capacity for genuine feeling—certainly a critical element in humanness—is what humanizes him. There is something, Algren seems to be saying, in post–World War II American society that induces guilt in everyone, including the middle class, which attempts to deny it by accumulating material possessions, a truly vicious circle since the guilt originates in their entrapment in the material, their alienation from anything spiritually redemptive. In contrast, urban grotesques such as Frankie and the Sparrow lack the resources necessary to obtain a protective layer of material possessions, of "things." They are trapped in "The great, secret and special American guilt of owning nothing, nothing at all, in the one land where ownership and virtue are one" (MGA, 19). They are moreover constantly reminded of this failing: "Guilt that lay crouched behind every billboard which gave each man his commandments; for each man here had failed the billboards all down the line. No Ford in this one's future nor ever any place all his own. Had failed before the radio commercials, by the streetcar plugs and by the standards of every self-respecting magazine" (MGA, 19). Frankie's abrupt shift from narrative detachment to existential guilt in this scene effectively undercuts the middle-class reader's need to distance himself from Frankie and the other residents of the ghetto. Frankie has abruptly become most painfully human, his fundamental humanness exposed, made naked, and thus impossible to deny. Algren's middle-class reader lives in a "third-person" society but is still a first-person human being trapped with all the others in a facticity that leads inexorably to death.

In order to emphasize further the essential humanness of the most grotesque citizens of the ghetto, Algren describes "an old wino" in the prison: "The old man . . . began a compulsive sort of scratching through the yellowed underwear, the fingers working with a life of their own, starting below the low sagging hill of the fallen thighs and laboring methodically upward as if pursuing the blood like a dog following its fleas; up over the hill and there paused, digging with blunted fingernails but yet without haste and even with something of pleasure . . . he seemed to be pacing himself, knowing just how long this job would require" (MGA, 21).

On the surface, it would seem difficult to find a more obvious example of Den Tandt's "twisted monstrosities"—trapped in an "urban slime"—than the old wino. He, in fact, seems not far from Jack London's "new and different race" of subhuman creatures. Algren deliberately portrays his compulsively repeating a grotesque, antisocial action precisely in order to accentuate his seeming lack of humanness. Initially, he must appear to the middle-class reader—who presumably is never reduced to obsessive scratching, at least not in public—as a grotesque, unclean creature not far removed from the roach. Certainly, the old wino is drowning—not in a water bucket but in his triple entrapment: in prison, in the material, in his own undirected and crippling guilt.

Yet, as in the passage describing Frankie and the roach, the scene insists on the old man's humanness. The wino repeats again and again to an uncaring audience that he "used to be night watchman on the old Wabash [railroad]" (MGA, 21). That job—one a middle-class reader would probably view contemptuously since it surely did not pay enough to permit the purchase of expensive material possessions or perhaps even a subscription to the *Saturday Evening Post*—nevertheless represents the one source of pride in the old man's life. As with his scratching, though, most of the other inmates have learned to ignore the wino's repeated assertion of self-worth. But not quite all of them. Humanized by his crippling guilt, Frankie, who longs to be a jazz drummer, understands the importance of such a personal declaration of individual worth, of human value. He tells the Sparrow: "That's a good job all the same. . . . You watch over people while they sleep. It's when everybody depends on you, nothin' bad should happen. . . . It's why you shouldn't laugh at some old guy if he's been a good night watcher" (MGA, 21).

Significantly, Frankie has shifted terms here: the old wino now was not a night watchman, but a night watcher. As has Frankie himself, he has watched the coming of the night, of death, in a futile attempt to stop it, to shut it out. Inevitably, he failed, and those he knew have all died, leaving him alone and forgotten: "'They don't remember people around here any more," he complained aloud at last'" (MGA, 22). Indeed, they don't, and the middle-class reader is shocked into an awareness that the night comes for everyone, that no amount of material possessions will ward it off, and that, after it comes, "they" will not remember anyone. A "twisted monstrosity"—even a "libidinal monster" at first glance—the old wino is human, no more and no less doomed than everyone else.

The novel's true climactic moment occurs when the "defrocked preacher" forces Record Head Bednar to an analogous realization. Throughout the novel, Algren has used Bednar as a stand-in for the implied privileged middle-class reader. Bednar attempts to isolate himself from awareness of his mortality by transforming his job into theater. The police lineup is the immediate arena in which his carefully constructed drama is enacted. He exhibits "suspects" to an audience of respectable middle-class voyeurs who are safely hidden behind a two-way mirror. As in the opening prison scene with Frankie and the Sparrow, he initiates a line of questioning for each "suspect" that is intended not to obtain information but to amuse a detached and condescending audience:

> [a "suspect" described as "a shock-haired razorback"]:
> Just throwed a rock at a wall 'n it happened to go through a window instead. So I followed through. But I didn't have no *in*tent of stealing.
>
> [Bednar]: You never have. But you're in and out like a fiddler's elbow all the same. What was the stretch in the Brushy Mountain pen for?
>
> [the "suspect"]: I got the wrong number was all.
>
> [Bednar]: I think you did. The wrong house number.
>
> [the "suspect"]: That's right. The people were home. I was drinking pretty heavy.
>
> [Bednar]: What do you do when you're drinking light?
>
> [the "suspect"]: Mind my own business.
>
> [Bednar]: You haven't got any business. For a quarter you'd steal the straw out of your mother's kennel. (MGA, 188)

For most of this scene, the reader shares a narrative perspective with Bednar's respectable audience, safely hidden behind the two-way mirror of the text and condescendingly enjoying the ritualized dehumanization of the "suspects." The perspective abruptly shifts, however, when the "defrocked preacher" "impales" Bednar by asserting, as a twentieth-century Walt Whitman, that "we are all members of one another" (MGA, 196). Forced to hear the truth of the "preacher's" message and acknowledge his bond with all the "suspects," who constitute humanity, Bednar abandons his theater. Most significantly, the words of the "preacher's" jolt the reader out from behind the two-way textual mirror and into the consciousness of Bednar; the reader is no longer protected from an awareness of his or her own "suspect" humanity. The theater ends; the game is over; Algren's complex aesthetic that affirms Den Tandt's "naturalist gothic" only to deny it with shocking immediacy is fully and unforgettably revealed. The scene switches abruptly from a theater of detachment to something reminiscent of Antonin Artaud's "theater of cruelty," in which the reader-audience is assaulted by the actions occurring on the stage of the text.

In *The Man with the Golden Arm*, Algren seems to go one better than Norris, London, and subsequent urban naturalists by making his urban "grotesques" absurd instead of menacing. He describes them in deliberately condescending language: "unincapable" punks, "the Republic's crummiest lushes," "patriot(s)" (MGA, 6, 18). Moreover, he has Frankie Machine kill Nifty Louie in an unpremeditated, almost offhand, manner. Here Frankie is no McTeague killing Trina to get her gold coins, no Bigger Thomas raping Bessie and then assaulting her with a brick. He is always a vulnerable "suspect" who commits a capital crime almost accidentally, almost as an afterthought; he is a powerless "habitual" caught in the absurd theater of his own destruction.

Notes

1. Christophe Den Tandt, *The Urban Sublime in American Literary Naturalism* (Urbana: University of Illinois, 1998), 34.

2. Ibid., 126.

3. Jack London, *The People of the Abyss* (1903; repr., London: Journeyman Press, 1977), 13.

4. June Howard, *Form and History in American Literary Naturalism* (Chapel Hill: University of North Carolina Press, 1985), 105.

5. Maxwell Geismar is correct in asserting that Frankie, as are many of Algren's characters, is, to a large degree, relieved to be in jail. Geismar describes

jail as an "iron sanctuary" that allows Frankie to escape his "fevered and distorted hopes." *American Moderns: From Rebellion to Conformity* (New York: Hill & Wang, 1958), 187.

6. Nelson Algren, *The Man with the Golden Arm: 50th Anniversary Critical Edition,* ed. William J. Savage Jr. and Daniel Simon (New York: Seven Stories Press, 1999), 6. Further references are to this edition and are cited parenthetically as MGA.

7. Den Tandt, *The Urban Sublime in American Literary Naturalism,* 127.

8. James R. Giles, *Confronting the Horror: The Novels of Nelson Algren* (Kent, Ohio: Kent State University Press, 1989), 56–72.

Textual Outlaws: The Colonized Underclass in Nelson Algren's *The Man with the Golden Arm*

Ian Peddie

IN *THE MAN WITH THE GOLDEN ARM* (1949) NELSON ALGREN'S characters move apparently oblivious to the machinations of the greater world outside the parameters of Division Street. Theirs is a world limited to the Tug & Maul Bar, the Safari Bar, the Division Street hotel, and Zero Schwiefka's gambling den. "On Skid Row," Algren writes, "even the native-born no longer felt they had been born in America. They felt they had merely emerged from the wrong side of its billboards."[1] The passage offers a useful departure point for analysis of Algren's novel and particularly of his protagonists, who, domiciled in the inegalitarian world of Division Street, find nothing more than a status quo founded upon iniquity, for "That was the way things were because that was how things had always been" (MGA, 7). Though such words have become something of a defining phrase for Algren's fiction, I suspect they constitute more of a sense of protest than of determinist acceptance.

In trying to get at some aspect of what condemns Algren's characters to such dreadful lives, I want to go back over forty-five years—back, in fact, to Blanche H. Gelfant's *The American City Novel*. In that volume, Gelfant's discussion of the sense of doom in *The Man with the Golden Arm* included the observation that Algren's characters are "islanded within a larger society." Here was a seam that was perhaps not open to investigation in the conservative-dominated cold war years, but Gelfant was onto something with this phrase, and she followed it up by suggesting that "organized society . . . condemns Skid Row while it shares the guilt for its existence."[2] As far as a brief summing up of *The Man with the Golden Arm* goes, this seems an accurate enough appraisal, and although Gelfant did not explore the thoughts, the thinking that prompted these and other similar phrases would become an integral part of the criticism of colonialism, and in that respect postcolonial criticism can throw considerable light on *The Man with the Golden Arm*. Having said that, I do not intend to engage in a blow-by-blow comparative analysis of the position of various colonized peoples around the world and those in Algren's novel. Rather, I want to use some of the initiatives postcolonial criticism has provided as a guide not so much to suggest that the degrees of oppression across colonial lines are simply comparable but, rather, to explore the reasons that the techniques of domination usually reserved for export can and do have remarkable domestic influence.

If, then, the protagonists of *The Man with the Golden Arm* are "islanded," it is the ubiquitous El that functions as the island's border. The El, of course, features strongly in a good deal of Algren's work, and it always performs the function of highlighting the city as a prison. For Bruno in *Never Come Morning* (1942), for example, the El offers the comfort of a place to sleep, though the refuge is tempered by the knowledge that the El remains the framework of the "cageworked city's curbs and walks."[3] In that respect, *The Man with the Golden Arm* is no different from Algren's earlier work, for when Sophie, from the prison of her wheelchair, looks out of a window, she sees "only how the city was bound, from southeast to the unknown west, steel upon steel upon steel: how all its rails held the city too tightly to the thousand girdered El" (MGA, 96). And as Frankie prepares for his death, "a Madison Street trolley" charges past "in a streamlined, cat-howling fury"—an event that gives him "an odd excitement," confirming that just as the El has been a symbol in his life, so it must also be a symbol of his death (MGA, 337).

Part of the reason the El holds such force in the novel is that it appears to offer hope for what postcolonial critics have called the "contact zone"—an area in which two or more cultures meet and engage in conflict such that each alters in response to the other. Yet despite its pervasive presence, no one in *The Man with the*

Golden Arm actually rides the El until Frankie's abortive attempt to escape at the novel's climax. Hence for Algren's characters, contact with cultures other than their fellow urban poor remains strictly limited, and other than Sophie's visits to Dr. Pasterzy, there is no cross-cultural contact in the novel. Instead, the characters have to make do with Captain Bednar—a crucial figure in the novel and one who in postcolonial terms functions as part of what might be called the colonial chain of command, a role that he himself ultimately begins painfully to recognize. In the postcolonial sense, Bednar is in fact an authorized colonial, undertaking the role of the mediating figure between the colonizers and the colonized. Daydreaming anxiously as he awaits the pleas of another detained suspect, Bednar envisages a scenario that rehearses many a colonial encounter:

> Only the captain, trapped between the hunters and the hunted, looked mournfully through that green steel door as though yearning to follow his innocents there.
>
> To follow each man to a cell all his own, there to confess the thousand sins he had committed in his heart.
>
> For he seemed to see them still, each with the left hand manacled and the right thrown protectively across the eyes.
>
> As his own left hand, in dreams, seemed cuffed, of late, to smooth cold steel. (MGA, 199)

There is no better way of understanding this than to recall E. M. Forster's complaint of "the undeveloped heart" of the British, which separated them not merely from the Indians over whom they ruled but also from each other, for Bednar too is separated—from his colleagues, from those he condemns. Yet slowly, Bednar begins to recognize the ambivalence of his position, and the pain his recognition causes is as important to the novel as the despair felt by those born on the wrong side of the billboards. By the same token, the captain's persistent doubts over whether he is the pursuer or the pursued is not only a thought that haunts him privately, for it has an overt political function in that it serves to indicate the harm colonialism can do to those in power. It was, of course, the defrocked priest's declaration that "we are all members of one another" (MGA, 198) that set the captain thinking. Yet by that time the captain already knew that something was amiss. As early as the novel's first page "the finger of guilt" had touched "the dark gray muscle behind the captain's light gray eyes" (MGA, 3), and as the novel progresses, so does the captain's perception. He begins to realize he is only a link in the chain of command, or, as Algren puts it, a "manacled" link (MGA, 296). He realizes he is only fulfilling the directives of the Division Street super and that he is only one perilous rung up from those he sends to the state prison. Seemingly unable to alter the situation, the captain repeatedly arrives at resolutions indicative of his own compromised position, one in which he is at the same time both guilty and helpless. Alone in the query room, for instance, the captain is "stifled by a ravaging guilt, [for] he knew now those whom he had denied, those beyond the wall, had all along been members of himself" (MGA, 298).

The captain's uneasiness over the priest's declaration that "we are all members of one another" stems from the phrase's implicit demand that he admit his similarities to the characters he condemns. In postcolonial terms, there has to be a sense of difference between colonizer and colonized, or the practice of colonialism might simply die out, and one of the captain's roles is to maintain and ensure that sense of difference. And despite being wracked with doubt about his role, the captain spends most of his time pointing up and sanctioning difference: "I know you," he [Bednar] thinks cunningly of the outlaws. "I know you. I know you all" (MGA, 199). Record Head's distancing of himself from the "outlaws"—a distancing that functions on social, cultural, and class levels—is an emphatic denial of what postcolonial critics have called a syncretic fusion between the self and the Other, and in this respect it echoes colonial attempts to maintain order and control.

Such is the captain's need to maintain difference that he is willing to construct the most bizarre visions in order to ensure it: "The captain's eyes went down the line. The masks were managing to change, slowly and ever so slyly, to look less like plastic men and more like some plastic zoo: animals stuffed for some State Street Toyland the week before Christmas. Here was the toothless tiger and here the timid lion, here the bull that loved flowers and there some lovelorn moose" (MGA, 193–94). In this example, it is almost as if the image of the colonial has become too close to that of the colonizer—a point that the postcolonial critic Homi K. Bhabha called the necessity of maintaining the presence of the colonized as "almost the same, but not quite"—and thus it must again be distanced.[4] Bednar certainly "knows" the outlaws, but he knows better still the need to articulate their very difference—a need driven by a coloniallike necessity to maintain power that while not devoid of an understanding of the implications of such power, ultimately denies it. The inappropriate images of the accused as a "toothless tiger," a "timid lion," a "bull that loved flowers," and a "lovelorn moose" say far more about Bednar and what he represents than they do about those standing in the dock. Because he recognizes his own sense of complicity in their downfall, Bednar needs to construct that difference despite the presence of physical weaknesses that mark almost every character in the novel. Frankie Machine, for example, "could never acknowledge that he squinted a bit. 'If anythin' was wrong with my peepers the army wouldn't of took me,' he argued, 'the hand is quicker than the eye—'n I got a *very* naked eye'" (MGA, 10). If the physical functions as a cultural signifier, then Frankie's squint marks his body as incongruous, and he, as is every other character in the novel, is as fetishized as the more extreme examples such as Blind Pig and Drunkie John. Superficial physical difference is, of course, only one sign of Frankie's problems, though it marks him and so many others in the novel as inferior. Algren's characters are, in fact, to Bednar, to society, and, as we shall see, to many critics the "impossible Other." Their physical difference functions in postcolonial terms as their "natural" inferiority and is consequently written into the ideology of difference, and this, I think, is an important issue that lies behind many critics' ready dismissal of Algren's work.

The various bodies on display in *The Man with the Golden Arm* are ascribed certain cultural significance that inculcates notions of difference on almost every level. That strategy, according to Abdul R. JanMohamed, permits a "rapid exchange of denigrating images which can be used to maintain a sense of moral difference. The ideological function of this mechanism," JanMohamed continues, in addition to prolonging colonialism, is to "dehistoricize and desocialize the conquered world, to present it as a metaphysical 'fact of life.'"[5] Here was a phrase with which Algren would have agreed, for his point was not to write of the urban poor out of what Chester Eisinger called his "sheer sentimental sympathy for the underdog"[6] but to explicitly question the legitimacy of a position wherein the awful existences of his characters could somehow be explained away merely in terms of their own corruption.

Despite the fact that Algren was wont to conclude that "Neither God, war, nor the ward super work any deep change on West Division Street" (MGA, 7), his narrativization of the methods and results of internal colonialism was nonetheless a sustained attempt to present a view of what Michael Harrington called "the other America."[7] Attempts to present a view from the other side—from the inside, in fact—are of course what make postcolonial literature so compelling. We might say the same about Algren's work, for just as the broad contours of postcolonial literature began to respond to political, social, and cultural imperatives that questioned established colonial histories, so Algren's work represents the American literary Left's need to alter its response to the changing times. When Algren wrote *The Man with the Golden Arm*, it was no longer acceptable to engage in the kind of revolutionary exhortations favored by Michael Gold and others in the 1930s. From about the time of the Hitler-Stalin pact, the American Left had to find alternate means of expression in order to survive. Hence, not only does Algren's work continue the social-protest tradition of the 1930s through questions of class, it also complicates it through the difficult merger of questions of class and ethnicity. And we might say that in twenty-first-century America, ethnicity and class are all but inseparable, for as Michael Denning puts it, "[T]he invention of ethnicity was a central form of class consciousness in the United States."[8] Algren, I suspect, recognized that, and though class and ethnicity function together as one of the central issues in *The Man with the Golden Arm*, the theme was lost on those critics who either could not or would not see what was at stake.

By 1963 Eisinger had decided that Algren was "indifferent to ideas" and, more bizarrely, that "his criticism of American life [was] not in any sense ideological" but resulted instead from a "compound of resentment and perversity."[9] The die had already been cast, and it was forged not through those reviews that found *The Man with the Golden Arm* "unforgettable"[10] and "one of the best novels of the year so far"[11] but through those based on the consensus that—to use Alfred Kazin's term—the characters were "freaks."[12] In fact, the critical and cultural consolidation of internal colonialism had already found fertile ground among a number of influential critics long before Eisinger accused Algren of "forcing things" upon readers.[13] Leslie A. Fiedler, in one of the more notorious reviews of Algren, felt secure in using the rhetoric of colonialism when he spoke of "The Noble Savages of Skid Row."[14] And in a piece entitled "The Man with the Golden Beef," Norman Podhoretz registered his "uneasiness" over *The Man with the Golden Arm*, a novel he felt could be dismissed because he had seen such characters before: had "previously observed the antics of their kind."[15]

Podhoretz found in Algren nothing but "bums and whores, hoboes and pimps, con men, and other outcasts." He didn't find any attempt of the author to question why people lived such fearful lives, and he concluded that Algren's characters "weren't worth the bother of following anyway."[16] The ideology implicit in such sentiments points to the worst of cold war myths about cultural homogeneity, which were no doubt to some extent promoted by the apparent absence of social consciousness among the small but powerful elite who gather around *Partisan Review*. What occurred was that in much the same way that social deviants have been traditionally "moved out" to the colonies, deviant opinion such as that found in *The Man with the Golden Arm* was also critically "moved out" to a colony beyond the center that was *Partisan Review* and its circle.

Unfortunately, such critics as Fiedler and Podhoretz were not alone. Critically at least, what had happened was that "new owners had moved in,"[17] as Algren puts it, though the old tenants remained. Few critics could recognize that the "old tenants" were singing the same song but, crucially, using a different tune. That failure to perceive the changing forms of expression on the Left meant that in much the same way, the captain was "manacled to his own unfiled arrest slips" (MGA, 296), so Algren, as are other characters in the novel, was "manacled by circumstance" (MGA, 196). The awful irony continues when we realize that the same could be said of Polish Americans—or any ethnic group, for that matter—struggling for existence in urban Chicago. From this perspective it is difficult to subscribe to Thomas Napierkowski's view that *The Man with the Golden Arm* "risks the danger of convincing that they are inferior."[18] Certainly, no one would deny that *The Man with the Golden Arm* is a novel about the wretched of Chicago's earth. But it is also a novel about much more than Polish Americans, in that it speaks not only for Frankie Machine and the Division Street regulars but also for Richard Wright's Bigger Thomas, for James T. Farrell's Studs Lonigan, for Willard Motley's Nick Romano.

The sense I get from the novel is that Algren's point is far more subtle than critics have realized. I am convinced that in *The Man with the Golden Arm* and throughout Algren's work, we need to embrace what postcolonial critics have long understood: that colonialism does damage not only to the colonized but also to the colonizer. If we accept that point, then we can move beyond disparaging descriptions of Algren's characters as "their kind" and "freaks" and see that the kind of institutionalized violence and ruthless social Darwinism sanctified in the name of colonialism are at the heart of *The Man with the Golden Arm*. To guide our way, the example of Captain Bednar's angst-ridden existence ought to be a caveat, for there are few more forceful examples of what colonialism can do even to those in power.

Algren once said that "the hard necessity of bringing the judge on the bench down into the dock has been the peculiar responsibility of the writer in all ages of man."[19] It was a felicitous comment from a writer who had spent his whole life illuminating injustice—no more so than in *The Man with the Golden Arm*—because for Algren, as for postcolonial writing, the relationship between society and its literature was intimate. Perhaps the best way of ending this essay is to give the final word to Algren's closing description of Captain Bednar, for despite myriad examples that indicate the awful lives all characters in *The Man with the Golden Arm* lead, I think the following offers the clearest example of the human cost of what I have called "internal colonialism." Bednar, Algren writes, "was unworthy of the lowliest—and there was no court to try any captain for doing his simple duty. No place was provided, by church or state, where such a captain might atone for everything he had committed in his heart. No judge had been appointed to pass sentence upon such a captain. He had been left to judge himself" (MGA, 298).

Notes

1. Nelson Algren, *The Man with the Golden Arm* (1949; repr., New York: Four Walls Eight Windows, 1990), 17. Further references are to this edition and are cited parenthetically as MGA.

2. Blanche H. Gelfant, *The American City Novel* (Norman: University of Oklahoma Press, 1954), 253.

3. Nelson Algren, *Never Come Morning* (1942; repr., New York: Seven Stories Press, 1987), 30.

4. Homi K. Bhabha, "Of Mimicry and Man: The Ambivalence of Colonial Discourse," *October* 28 (1984): 126.

5. Abdul R. JanMohamed, "The Economy of Manichean Allegory: The Function of Racial Difference in Colonist Literature," *Critical Inquiry* 12, no. 1 (1985): 67.

6. Chester Eisinger, *Fiction of the Forties* (Chicago: University of Chicago Press, 1963), 75.

7. See Michael Harrington, *The Other America: Poverty in the United States* (Harmondsworth, England: Penguin, 1962).

8. Michael Denning, *The Cultural Front: The Laboring of American Culture in the Twentieth Century* (London: Verso, 1997), 238.

9. Eisinger, *Fiction of the Forties,* 74.

10. Hollis Alpert, "Fallen Angels," *Saturday Review*, October 8, 1949, 32.

11. "The Lower Depths," *Time*, September 12, 1949, 104–5.

12. Alfred Kazin, "Some People Passing By," *New York Times Book Review*, May 20, 1956, 24.

13. Eisinger, *Fiction of the Forties,* 80.

14. Leslie A. Fiedler, "The Noble Savages of Skid Row," *The Reporter*, January 12, 1956, 43-44.

15. Norman Podhoretz, "The Man with the Golden Beef," *New Yorker*, June 2, 1956, 132.

16. Ibid., 133.

17. Nelson Algren, introduction to *The Neon Wilderness* (1947; repr., New York: Hill & Wang, 1960).

18. Thomas Napierkowski, "The Image of Polish Americans in American Literature," *Polish American Studies* 40 (Spring 1983): 18.

19. Nelson Algren, *Chicago: City on the Make* (1951; repr., Chicago: University of Chicago Press, 1983), 83.

The City That Turned the White Sox Black: Post–World War II Chicago Boosterism and the Negation of Nelson Algren

Caroline Gottschalk-Druschke

CHICAGO READERS AND CIVIC BOOSTERS RECEIVED NELSON ALGREN'S 1951 *Chicago: City on the Make* as an embarrassing attack on a city they clamored to repair and reshape in the economic upturn that followed World War II. Conservative reviewers and Chicago power brokers utilized the booming economy and rising conservatism of the era to boost interest in the city from within and without. In that climate, Algren's aim to textually represent the symbiotic tensions inherent to Chicago undermined the proud city of feeling that Chicago's civic boosters had fostered through political, cultural, and economic change. Those civic boosters and politicians worked to cast Chicago as a thriving capital of economy and tourism and refused to incorporate Algren's representation of the city's checkered past. Algren saw the glory of Chicago in its scams and alleyways while economically advantaged and powerful Chicagoans struggled to forget the city's murky past. In *Chicago*, Algren captures and elucidates the nature of the historically layered city in his rich and balanced tones of gray. The recuperating postwar Chicago denied Algren's textual city because of the threat they recognized in Algren's aims.

Americans on the brink of 1950 eagerly anticipated the dawn of the new decade, one of limitless opportunity and the chance to forget their war-tinged memories of the economic instability and depression of the first half of the century. For the first time, a broad group of Americans pursued higher education and had the leisure time to enjoy the economic boom. Glossy travel and lifestyle magazines appealed to Americans with expendable income, and in 1951 one such magazine commissioned Algren to write a piece on Chicago. A local writer who had gained renown when his *The Man with the Golden Arm* (1949) won the first National Book Award the previous year, Algren emerged as the natural choice for the magazine piece. After an initial reading, *Holiday* editors deemed Algren's essay out of sync with the aims of a traditional travel magazine and so published a highly edited version of the essay—to Algren's dismay. Glossy magazines of the 1950s worked to sell products and services in the postwar economic upswing, and Algren's essay did nothing to sell Chicago to the rest of the nation. Doubleday publishers capitalized on Algren's frustration with *Holiday* and offered to release the piece in book form at roughly the same time. More intense than *Holiday*'s watered-down version, Algren's prose poem *Chicago* was unfurled on Chicago and the rest of America in October 1951.

While *Chicago* received favorable initial reviews from New Yorkers, many Chicago readers were stunned by the book. A *Chicago Daily News* reviewer proclaimed the piece "A Case for Ra(n)t Control,"[1] and while the *Chicago Sun-Times* praised the book, it did so anonymously.[2] Chicago's postwar civic boosters found themselves unable to accept or appreciate such an all-inclusive portrait of the city. With the World War II years and the previous Depression fresh in their memory, Chicago politicians saw the booming postwar economy as an opportunity to encourage an optimistic boost to civic pride. Given the climate of optimism, the book did not sell. Not only that, but "furious boosters struck back with a vengeance" against Algren's inclusion of the aspects of Chicago they tried to dismiss.[3] This particular Chicago audience could not afford Algren's aim to capture the spirit of his city in both its bright points and its darker undertones.

Algren presented the historical corruption and despair permeating Chicago's varied past to enhance a richly gray understanding of the city. From its very inception, the factual Chicago blossomed from betrayal. Algren's textual city necessarily includes notorious characters such as Chicago's swindler forefathers, who "paid the Pottawattomies off in cash in the cool of the Indian evening and had the cash back to the dime by the break of the Indian dawn" (CCM, 12). Pavement-colored light, filthy tenements, and blatant injustice pervade the gritty Chicago captured in portions of the essay, yet *Chicago*, however brutal, is not a one-sided piece. Algren tellingly begrudged the reviewer who asserted, "A more partial, distorted, unenviable slant was never taken by a man pretending to cover the Chicago story" (CCM, 88), precisely because his text is so deliberately two-sided. Algren realized that the only true way to represent his Chicago was to include all sides, all inhabitants, and all truths. Algren is sure to include the likes of Hinky Dink Kenna: "part philanthropist and part straight brigand" (CCM, 20); "Like the city that bred him, he had a heavenly harpist on his bedpost as well as a hustler's imp stoking the furnace" (CCM, 20), for Chicago is a city where "always our villains have hearts of gold and all our heroes are slightly tainted" (CCM, 21). Algren bestowed on the reader his own knowledge of the city—both skid row and the Gold Coast—and thereby captured the symbiotic city he meant to reflect. But if Algren succeeded in capturing this city, there were very few at the time who wanted it captured. Algren's Chicago came to life in a deep and shadowy gray, wedged between the ivory towers and the El track shadows, and therein lay *Chicago*'s damaging truth.

In carefully balanced prose, Algren revealed his beloved to his audience. Far from ignoring the glory of the city, Algren recognized its true beauty in its balance. He sang the praises of this disparate city while immediately structuring the narrative on the basis of balance. In the opening lines of the text, the reader is physically placed at the center of a city balancing in the middle of two very different sides. *Chicago* opens with the passage "To the east were the moving waters as far as eye could follow. To the west a sea of grass as far as wind might reach" (CCM, 10). Just as there are two key sides to Chicago geographically, physically, politically, and culturally, there are two sides to Algren's prose. Both are key to understanding the enriching, varied tones of a many-hued city: to deny any one side is to deny the whole. Chicago is balanced between lake and prairie in much the same way as Algren's prose representation is balanced on the brink of a much larger cultural shift. The wealthy and powerful Chicagoans who denied Algren's work abandoned their city views for the suburban prairie or skyscraping lake views. That denial of the many-layered city mirrored the denial of Algren's prose. As Chicagoans struggled to reinvent the postwar city for themselves as a place of limitless opportunity, they denied the necessity of Algren's notion that Chicago was great precisely because of its limitations and checkered past.

Chicago's denial of Algren's textual city is unfortunate in that he embraces the muddy history of the city in *Chicago* because an understanding of that history is essential to an understanding of the present-day city. Algren describes his relationship with Chicago as "loving a woman with a broken nose, you may well find lovelier lovelies. But never a lovely so real" (CCM, 23). Algren's personification of Chicago implies that traditional beauty is out of context in an appreciation of Chicago. If history and meaning are more essential than beauty to love, then Algren establishes his credentials in his love for the dichotomy of the city, having walked the streets and the alleys in both the morning and the night. This is a Chicago with two distinct faces: "One for the sunlit traffic's noontime bustle. And one for midnight subway watches when stations swing past like ferris wheels of light, yet leave the moving window wet with rain or tears" (CCM, 23–24). The very landscape of the city that sprang up between the moving waters of the east and the western sea of grass, built "by old-world hands with new-world tools" (CCM, 48), fosters that duality. The gray history and landscape of Chicago require balanced perspectives. Unfortunately, the passage of time has witnessed a readership that largely recognizes only the dark elements of *Chicago* and so dismisses Algren's telling of Chicago in the textual city that he created.

That conservative Chicago readership would misunderstand not only Algren's prose but also the purpose of the piece as a whole. The political, cultural, and social powers in Chicago refused to accept that Algren's textual city captured the city's mood. Considering the immense task of selling Chicago to itself and the rest of the nation in the new postwar economy, Algren's *Chicago* damaged the Chicago that civic boosters toiled to project. The textual city created by Algren threatened the revenue that could be gained from increased tourism and civic participation in negating the efforts of politicians and civic boosters. The peculiar dichotomy of Chicago lay in its symbiotic tension of the North Side and the South Side, Catholic and Protestant, German and Irish, but to represent Chicago to the world in 1950 as the textual Chicago that Algren captured in *Chicago* meant economic and political trouble. In 1950, the potential for readers outside a certain frame of reference—the city of fact shaped by experience and feeling—to appreciate Algren's aims was slight. The threat of Algren's prose lay in its potential corruption of America's view of the Chicago of fact.

In Chicago, specifically, the local government, ruled by the figurehead Martin Kennelly from 1947 to 1955 and by machine head Richard J. Daley from 1955 on, directed the massive postwar expansion and restructuring of the city. Politicians and business interests altered Chicago throughout those years in the same boost of civic pride, greed, and denial that drove the conservative changes in America as a whole. Algren's textual Chicago damaged the city that Kennelly and, later, Daley fought to rebuild and reshape. While Algren used *Chicago* to represent his multifaceted city to the public, his conservative audience dismissed his attempts as damaging in his representations of crime and corruption. Chicago civic leaders hoped to leave Al Capone and the Haymarket riots behind them, submerging Chicago's muddy history in hopes for a brighter future. This government further fostered the dismissal of Chicago's less-appealing elements through a strict regimen of dividing the physical city and, in so doing, divided the city of emotion and feeling. Division in Chicago was so pervasive that the columnist Mike Royko commented, "Containing the Negro was unspoken policy in those days," and "Even the expressways were planned as man-made barriers."[4] Those divisions necessarily influenced the attitudes of people within the city. The Chicago captured in Algren's text, while in portions beautiful and glorious, had still been built on a hustle. The postwar Chicago civic boosters, eagerly dividing themselves and their city—with the help of federal policy—from a past they wished to disavow, had no emotional capacity to assimilate those damaging memories into a cohesive picture of the city they wished to sell. With the weight of ancient scandals crumbling the sterile tourist image championed by civic boosters, Chicago advocates chose to deny the truth of Algren's work. In the spirit of progress, that truth constituted too much damage for them to absorb.

The peculiar economic and political climate in the later half of the twentieth century left power disparately concentrated in the hands of a privileged few, and this elite group sculpted the cultural face of America. Victory in World War II had left the American government in a position of overwhelming political strength and societal control. Howard Zinn noted that for the American government, the postwar boom in the economy generated "enough prosperity for enough of the population to ensure against the rebellions that so threatened the thirties"[5] while the atmosphere of crisis and cold war championed by the Truman Administration bred a massive rightward shift in political views, economic spending, and cultural capital. Conservatives and liberals rallied behind the anticommunist bandwagon that Zinn also notes "meant trouble for those who stayed outside the coalition as radical critics."[6] An intelligent and talented writer, Algren was precisely the type of intellectual targeted by McCarthy era—and pre–McCarthy era—America. Algren, in his notoriety and his inclusion of both the complete history of Chicago and the underprivileged elements in the city, was talented enough to potentially damage and discredit the image of Chicago that civic boosters and local politicians worked to project. Algren released *Chicago* to a reading public that was already showing strong signs of the rampant conservatism to come. Such an imbalance of power rendered Algren's textual city a threat to the larger conservative forces in America as well as an irritant to the privileged Chicagoans who had built and enforced the physical and emotional barriers of the city.

In their haste to disassociate themselves further from their grim past—and the infringing black population—affluent white Chicagoans fled to the suburbs during the 1950s in record numbers. They flocked across the physical borders of the city as a mental escape and fled the city, "fleeing all the things that suburbanites fled in the 1950s: landlords and cooking smells, neighbors one flight above or uncomfortably close next door, and physical surroundings that carried indelible reminders of hard times years before. They were giving up the grayness of Chicago for the pastels of DuPage County."[7]

They fled the very situations that colored Algren's prose and so fled the text itself. *Chicago* disturbed many readers and Chicago image makers in that, "For most readers, his [Algren's] world is a landscape we lack either the words or the desire to find familiar."[8] These readers could not rationally judge the merits of Algren's text as Algren's aims opposed their own. Chicago politicians in the 1950s aimed to clean up the city's image in attempts to make the city more appealing. Algren's aim to capture the symbiotic balance of Chicago threatened the denial that fueled the suburban flight and urban renewal. Emotionally and economically, Algren's city stood in direct conflict with the "new" Chicago.

While Algren accurately portrayed Chicago as a city whose dualities feed off one another, Chicago readers could not appreciate that inherent tension. With the majority of Chicago readers and spenders in denial, civic boosters realized that no one within the city could gain from Algren's truths, while no one outside the city could likely appreciate the precarious tension of Algren's textual Chicago. Algren understood and represented the dichotomous elements of the city as mutually necessary for the survival of each other: there would be no ivory towers without Chicago's grime-covered slums. The Chicago power brokers, however, had no use for Algren's work in their quest to present a new, bright, hope-filled postwar Chicago. That audience, busy dividing itself from the rest of society, chose to look away from an author who refused to do so.

The motives behind such a reception to *Chicago* are perhaps most easily understood in retrospect. America continued the right-ward lurch that began in the years immediately after World War II. Algren confronted that dramatic shift in his 1961 afterword to *Chicago*, in which he paralleled the accusatory political climate of post–World War II America with the lukewarm critical reception of his work. Cold war politics and the imminent threat of economic and cultural dissolution rendered nervous an American audience that dismissed *Chicago*'s multifaceted and many-toned clarity in their discomfort.

By 1960, fifteen years after the end of World War II, conservative forces controlled the political scene and ruled virtually every aspect of American life. The strong central government imposed divisions and controls on the American public, and the public, in large part, accepted the new status quo. Many Americans believed restraints on individual freedom were necessary defenses against the poison of Communism, and those who did not typically remained powerless. The thriving military defense industry necessitated an increase in labor and the resulting jobs and domestic economic stability justified government demand for optimistic—if not ignorant—support of the American government, its programs, and its reforms. This conservative and divided public could not tolerate the textual city represented in Algren's politically inspired prose. Algren qualified his representation of Chicago when he declared in his 1961 afterword to *Chicago*, "I submit that literature is made upon any occasion that a challenge is put to the legal apparatus by conscience in touch with humanity" (CCM, 81). The anti-communist elements in America, inspired by the first major economic upswing of the past half-century, could not risk accepting the type of city that Algren praised in *Chicago*. Algren's readership had dismissed the textual Chicago he had presented to the world in 1951, and in the wake of all of the time and money put toward civic boosterism, Algren's textual city threatened the textual Chicago that the city's leaders wanted to create.

If reviewers and Chicago cultural powers denied Algren's prose upon its debut in 1951, the ensuing years were no kinder to his work. By 1960, the establishment of the American post–World War II canon, combined with the changing face of the American city and the anti-communist shift, had garnered enough societal force to prompt complete dismissal of Algren's work. In a definitive work on American canons, Richard Ohmann says that during that time frame "people were responsive to novels where they discovered the values in which they believed" and includes Saul Bellow's observation that "what Americans want to learn from their writers is how to live."[9] America, by 1960, by no means wanted to live the life portrayed in Algren's work. Championing the view of Algren as a relic or reactionary, Leslie A. Fiedler assaulted the author as "isolated from the life of his time . . . our literature has moved on and left him almost a museum piece."[10] Norman Podhoretz spurned Algren's purposely balanced prose, citing that "the lyric and the sordid tend to cancel each other out, leaving only a vague sense of uplift and a dim aura of prettiness, as though Pollyanna were writing *The Grapes of Wrath* in dactylic hexameters."[11] Cultural forces, by this time, had pushed Algren to the brink of popularly and academically accepted literature. His writing neither suited the needs of civic boosters nor seemingly lived up to the expectations of the elitist reader or the elitist reviewer. Reviews by Fiedler and Podhoretz, combined with the force of the Daley machine, washed Algren completely from the picture. America, by the mid-1960s, had no use for the city of fact and feeling that Algren aimed to convey.

While a handful of critics now praise *Chicago*, few seem to grasp its intentional balance and its relevance to the living city. Bill Beuttler notes, "Algren knew he would catch heat for ignoring Chicago's prouder features."[12] Yet Algren does not ignore those features; he incorporates them into a more-cohesive whole. Though these passages are tempered by seedier images of the city, Algren includes the "white-and-blue miles of our beaches, the Saturday night moonlit excursions to Michigan City, the afternoon at the zoo washed into mists of sunlit remembrance by a sudden warm, still rain" (CCM, 24). In the eyes of many critics, the darker political and criminal elements of Algren's prose depiction of Chicago outweigh and overshadow its beauty. The Algren scholar Carlo Rotella recognizes those darker elements and notes the significance of *Chicago* mainly in its strength as a narrative of decline. Rotella sees Algren in 1951 as aiming to incorporate and convey aspects of a crumbling way of life. He sees that "the poem's great project is to show how and why the narrator's subject is disappearing,"[13] and yet Rotella's interpretation is missing a certain layer of understanding. Algren included enough triumphant aspects of his city to necessitate a more-balanced reading of the text itself. Algren may have thrown up his hands on the city in his 1961 afterword to the piece but did so after ten years of harsh critical reviews and drastic political change. *Chicago* elucidates the symbiotic elements that will continue to shape and create Chicago throughout the twentieth century and beyond. If, in Rotella's view, the city of fact and the city of feeling are mutually influential, then perhaps *Chicago* is a narrative of decline only due to the brutal response it evoked from the public. The negative reactions of Algren's audience recast the piece as unnecessary and unwanted in their modern city. Their response, rather than the text itself, marks the essay as one of decline. The city of feeling created by the factual changes of conservative America and the Daley machine deemed Algren's piece inauthentic and irrelevant, capturing an out-of-date city. Yet Algren laid down instructions for the Chicago reader in his crisp portrayal of the shaping forces and tensions within the city. While Algren chronicled the decline of the ethnic urban village, he placed that decline in the context of a larger Chicago history. The face of the city may have changed after World War II, but the underlying powers that shape the city have not. Regardless of Algren's feelings on the piece in retrospect, *Chicago* becomes a narrative of decline only when the cultural, political, and economic forces in Chicago and in the increasingly conservative nation decree that the piece is irrelevant to their world.

Ultimately, Algren's aims in the creation of *Chicago*'s textual city antagonized civic boosters in their attempts to reshape postwar Chicago. In their struggle to recast Chicago as an economic and tourist hub, politicians and big-business interests relied on the surging optimism and economic support of a highly conservative national audience. Those influential powers deemed Algren's text —which elucidated the symbiotic nature of the city—contrary to their needs. Despite the work's enduring relevance to the living city of fact and feeling, the increasing conservatism of the resulting years and debilitating reviews signaled the end for any possibility of acceptance into the popular or scholarly canon of the latter half of the twentieth century. The major literary powers of the day attacked Algren's credibility and talent, while the economic pressure to boost civic pride rendered Algren's textual city unwanted. Civic boosters struggled to create a precise Chicago of feeling that Algren's text threatened. The city of feeling that *Chicago*'s text had the capacity to create disputed the city championed by civic boosters, and as a result, Algren's textual city was rejected.

Notes

1. Nelson Algren, *Chicago: City on the Make* (1951; repr., Chicago: University of Chicago Press, 2001), 87. Further references are to this edition and are cited parenthetically as CCM.

2. Taken from an undated clipping in Algren's "Scrapbook," Ohio State University, Rare Books and Manuscripts.

3. Bill Beuttler, "Chicago in Their Sights," Chicagomag.com. March 2001 (http://www.billbeuttler.com/work28.htm) (accessed August 16, 2006), 1.

4. Mike Royko, *Boss, Richard J. Daley of Chicago* (New York: Signet, 1971), 137.

5. Howard Zinn, *A People's History of the United States* (New York: New Press, 1997), 311.

6. Ibid., 313.

7. Alan Ehrenhalt, *The Lost City: Discovering the Forgotten Virtues of Community in the Chicago of the 1950s* (New York: Basic Books, 1995), 197.

8. Daniel Simon, afterword to *Nonconformity: Writing on Writing*, by Nelson Algren (New York: Seven Stories Press, 1996), 92.

9. Richard Ohmann, "The Shaping of a Canon: U.S. Fiction, 1960–1975," *Critical Inquiry* 10, no. 1 (1983): 201.

10. Leslie A. Fiedler, "The Noble Savages of Skid Row," *The Reporter*, January 12, 1956, 43.

11. Norman Podhoretz, "The Man with the Golden Beef," *New Yorker*, June 2, 1956, 132.

12. Beuttler, "Chicago in Their Sights," 3.

13. Carlo Rotella, *October Cities: The Redevelopment of Urban Literature* (Berkeley: University of California Press, 1998), 23.

Nelson Algren and Carnival in 1930s America

Philip McGowan

ACROSS HIS FICTIONAL WORKS, NELSON ALGREN MAINTAINED A continuing interest in the realms of visuality and of the carnival locations in the United States. Once a hired hand at a county fair in the Rio Grande Valley in Texas, Algren shadows William Lindsay Gresham in his personal knowledge of American carnivals and their midway attractions of "the strong boy and the freaks and the girlie show and the cat with two hearts and so forth."[1] While acknowledging this as a recurrent theme throughout Algren's fictions, here the focus is *A Walk on the Wild Side* (1956) because of its concentration on the inversions, maskings, and displacements of a cultural impulse I want to define as American carnival. The last novel published in his lifetime, *A Walk on the Wild Side* was severely attacked by critics at the time of its publication but defended by Algren, who regarded it as his best work. James R. Giles notes both its subtheme of literacy and sex and the way it shadows Mark Twain's *The Adventures of Huckleberry Finn* (1884), reading Dove Linkhorn as an "ironic counterpart" to Twain's adolescent hero.[2] Dove, though, is a character of illusion and mock innocence, and any associations with Twain's novel are clearly parodic. For example, in place of Huck's irreligious and drunken father figure stands the drinking preacher Fitz, who excoriates Dove's brother, Byron, in staged weekly sermons of abuse and damnation before a regular crowd of townspeople. Arroyo is the now-vanished starting point and final destination for Dove in a novel of bawdy sexuality and carnal excess. Sex and power are two constants of the carnival realms he visits, where interpretation and authority are sited in penetration and repeated spectacle. Dove's ultimate success will occur as the brothel performer Big Stingaree, a sexual predator in staged peep shows, in acts in which sex is put on show for an audience of voyeuristic males. Unlike European systems of carnival, such performed sexuality is not a symbolic outlet suggestive of fertility rituals of rejuvenation in this region; instead, it is inserted into an economy of repeated performance and visual display. A novel of bawdy sexuality at one level and thus in keeping with the Rabelaisian universe of European carnival, *A Walk on the Wild Side* is an intriguing introduction to the world and cultural politics of American carnival.[3]

For the purposes of this discussion of Algren, American carnival is not a cultural phenomenon that is registered by yearly events, by self-contained temporal or spatial moments, or designated by religious rituals or festive celebrations. As a critical term it resists similar categorization to Bakhtinian definitions of carnival as a time out of time dissociated from the regular interactions of the social and cultural life of a country and its culture. Moreover, American carnival is not delimited to particular arenas or circus tents and cages, even though its most tangible manifestations are those of the freak show, or of American side-show culture. Rather, American carnival is a cultural phenomenon read as a term connoting the capacity of United States culture to employ a mode and method of seeing that operates along contours of race, ethnicity, and Otherness. American carnival is an interpretive and representative phenomenon activated at both the conscious and subconscious levels to consolidate white identity and, simultaneously, the very Otherness it seeks to exclude. These policies of exclusion are interspun with a particularized politics of exhibition and display: Otherness becomes both neutralized and glamorized by the activities of American carnival. For instance, the negation of the perceived perversion of color identity is operated through a process that seeks to embellish and exaggerate, in other words, to color intensely, the Otherness, the nonwhiteness that "regular" society moves to occlude. Such occlusion from systems of regular social interaction is made manifest by the maskings, distortions, and falsifications of identity that are intimately connected to the processes of carnival. The individual subjectivity of the Other is overwritten, blacked out, by a cultural recourse to generalized masks and stereotypes of identity. The introduction of critical debates concerning the nature and meaning of whiteness formulated by Toni Morrison, and continued by others such as Valerie Babb and Mike Hill, has opened a seam of cultural inquiry within the field of American literature, broadening the terms of engagement within readings of race to include considerations of white identity.[4]

The project of American carnival, originating with and maintained by the racial segregations formed by white America, resists all-inclusive readings of race, withholding white identity outside the sphere of racial or abnormal spectacle as both its spectator and the manipulator of its spectacular impact. American carnival is run through by its own particular color line that sections off whiteness from perceived threats to its social, economic, and cultural hegemony. The opportunities and potentials for what Mikhail Bakhtin terms *becoming* (the social, economic, or individual development that he outlines with regard to Rabelaisian carnival) are repackaged in American carnivals, restricted solely to white audience members and closed off from the Others on display. The exhibited identities are encased in a constricted mode of imagery that maintains their difference over time and replicates the salient features of their difference by the staging of repeated displays and performances throughout the year and across the nation's geographies. Their performance of Otherness is scripted and costumed by the requirements of the white proprietor and viewer and by the stereotyped perceptions of difference abroad in the wider culture. The impulse toward this form of carnival representation is one that reads difference through a lens of carnival identity. It is not an equating and democratic practice; on the contrary, American carnival is a cultural device that insists on categorizing difference. It is abroad within the culture and is deployed on particular overt occasions—world's fairs, P. T. Barnum's Museum of America, freak shows, each of them out of sync with European rhythms of carnival in line with feasts and seasonal cycles—to display Otherness and un-Americanness.

The placing of the subversive on display—in freak shows from the 1850s or in suggested forms of social, and particularly visual, punishment in the eras of temperance and Prohibition reform,[5] for example—is a technique employed to highlight the so-called normality of the rest of United States society. Difference—whether racial, cultural, or physical—is systematically reproduced and represented as alterity[6]; such displays of the absolutely different operate to confirm the racial, cultural, and physical regularity of American whiteness. The carnival and the American sideshow function via thc generalized stereotypes of blackness, ethnic identity, drunkenness, and so on, that obscure the individuality of the Others that white America seeks to overwrite. They also serve to rejuvenate mainstream culture by exhibiting the subversive in extrasocial arenas, locked cages, or ritualized festivals of identity construction. Georges Bataille's contention that "[m]onsters . . . would be the dialectical opposites of geometric regularity"[7] identifies the cultural territory particular to American carnival: the spectacular display of "monstrosity" in the confirmation of regular and "normal" American identity. Indeed, with regard to America's contributions to the spreading exposition culture—begun in 1851 with the Crystal Palace Exhibition in London and through its development of the world's fairs—it is evident that these showcase events provided an opportunity to advertise the advances made by American industry, science, and culture while incorporating highly carnivalized interpretations of nonwhiteness, un-Americanness, and Otherness within their carnival halls.

Such monological taxonomies of spectacle and display produce a transgressive and perceived subjective alterity that simultaneously legitimizes the normalized whiteness of fair spectators among the fee-paying public. As Peter Stallybrass and Allon White outline: "[R]acism, sexism, and xenophobia depend on the same production of the monster. Unconscious anxiety and compensating aggressive mockery are characteristic of all these discourses. In other words, the monster is a product of monological sublimation, whether this resonates with the self as an 'alien' contamination, or whether it is perceived as an external foreign body."[8] The democratic sense that is central to Bakhtin's delineation of carnival is certainly a collective one in which the identity of each living and breathing soul is recognized in the very functionality and physicality of their existence: "Carnival is not a spectacle seen by the people; they live in it, and everyone participates because its very idea embraces all the people."[9] In the United States, on the other hand, there is an absenting of any such culture of carnival laughter and forgetting. The binaries established through this particular culture and politics of seeing, as evinced in America's carnival spaces, do not call for or permit laughter; rather, they insist upon the categorization and the cataloging of difference. In American carnival, individualized identity becomes subsumed within a social structure that seeks to homogenize society by way of race, gender, and class readings that result in the displacement of unacceptable Otherness recognized in the construction of stereotyped masks of color, class, creed, and gender, such as minstrelsy and monstrosity. United States society constructs its own versions of carnival identities but implants them within the mundane and insistently noncarnival moments of daily interaction. The spaces of American carnival are internal in this culture and implicit within it: they are not externalized and random occurrences of irregularity or difference. Such carnival is not then an annual phenomenon or event; rather, it is a social code of systematized readings that operate in the production of color-coded, race-coded, class-coded, and gender-coded difference within American society. American carnival is clearly an alternative register to that outlined by Bakhtin: rather than being the centrifugal, decentralizing impulse he identifies in *Rabelais and His World*, American carnival's primary impulse is centripetal—toward a centralized and homogeneous reading of society and its cultural hierarchies. It does not seek to overthrow the dominant hegemony, instead functioning in support of the monologics of its single narrative of materialist success and white, male, middle-class identity. What is deemed freakish or subversive is displaced by this political vision of the United States and rehoused in its spaces and theaters of display.

Given such a reconception of the idea of carnival in the United States, it becomes clear that the spaces and moments of American carnival serve a dual function: to displace and simultaneously to display Otherness, to place non-American, un-American identities beyond regular social interaction and social viewing and exhibit them within extrasocial arenas that operate in the establishment of a politics of seeing, a visual economy of observing Otherness, blackness, "subversiveness."[10] The inference of political and economic registers here is not accidental: the entrance fee into America's carnival locations, be they sideshows, freak shows, minstrel shows, or the midway concessions of world's fairs, provided an economic sanction that facilitated the production and reproduction of such stereotyped versions of identity. This is not to claim, however, that white identity was excluded from the dioramas on view. On the contrary, the place of whiteness, of white achievement and advancement, particularly in the exhibits on display in the world's fairs, was one of racial superiority, but which was also necessarily entered into such staged manipulations of identity construction. Hierarchized as the optimum in cultural and racial identity, whiteness at the fairs was maintained as a distinct and autonomous entity, segregated from potential contaminating contact with deemed inferior races. The growing field of interest in decoding the manifestations of whiteness within American cultural representations, for example, in the work of Morrison and Babb, provides access to new readings of this previously unexamined face of American identity.

Algren's *A Walk on the Wild Side* may initially appear distantly placed from American world's fair culture, for example, but the narrative enacts a localized version of the cultural politics of American carnival seeing. As part of a white American underclass living in the dust bowl regions of Texas at the beginning of the 1930s, Dove Linkhorn is fostered in a male environment of abuse and violence, ultimately figured in his rape of Terasina Vidavarri. Dove's whiteness is not a privileged version of American identity; nor does it exhibit itself as vibrant or authoritative. Indeed, his "thinness of color"[11] becomes the base for later disguises and performances on the way to, and while in, New Orleans. His hometown of Arroyo is a border territory between East and West as well as between North and South. It is a liminal space of inactivity, unemployment, and forgotten myths of American progress. Time has been reversed here, and the suspension of reality transfers this place beyond the jurisdictions and calibrations of regular America. As the remainder of the novel intimates, Arroyo is not the only American town or city to suffer this fate during the Depression.

The linked performances around which Algren structures this novel are invariably anchored in costumed or masked identities. Without equivocation, however, these are not participants in carnivals of laughter. Performance, particularly sexual, is a contested territory, a space of opposition and domination controlled by white males as either observers, protagonists, or pimps. Even within marriage, sex is delineated as an arena of disguise and power: Terasina's former husband, a former army lieutenant, forces her on their wedding night to participate in a militaristic fantasy of whipping and abasement. Her later denial of Dove's own carnal urges results in the further sexual assault of rape; it becomes clear that the localities of Algren's fiction are mapped as cruel and uncompromising zones for satisfying male desire on demand. Abuse, physical and sexual, of women in this novel is unremitting: Kitty Twist recounts the beatings and markings she endured at the hands of men; each of the prostitutes in New Orleans is caught in an unending cycle of degraded behavior; even Hallie, who, it appears, can make the fairy-tale story of the tin soldier (taught to Dove by Terasina) come true, is under the control of Schmidt, a onetime carnival strong man who has lost his legs in a train accident. When the local economic situation deteriorates to the point that a coal train must be robbed of its stocks, the death of an anonymous girl (who clutches a Kewpie doll to her chest), dragged under the wheels of the train, indicates perpetual and arbitrary devastations of the female in the world of *A Walk on the Wild Side*.

As Schmidt's injuries suggest, women are not the only ones to suffer in the grotesque carnival environments of the novel. Schmidt's blinding of Dove in the climactic fight scene and his own death at the hands of the spectators afterward signal the incorporation and American adaptation of carnival events from medieval European traditions within routine American locations. Bakhtin notes how the grotesque and distorted body could become both a spectacular and a narrative event through "a long and detailed anatomic list of wounded members, organs, broken bones, and joints."[12] Algren's boxing fictions—particularly "The Face on the Barroom Floor" from the story collection *The Neon Wilderness* (1947), and this fight scene in *A Walk on the Wild Side*—narrate the abuse and destruction of the human form in ways analogous to Bakhtin's readings, but with the notable exemption of the rejuvenative capacities of humor. However, certain aspects of carnival overlapping Bakhtin's readings of François Rabelais are contained here. The New Orleans of this text is undoubtedly a carnal zone revelatory of the grotesqueries within the carnival spirit of United States social and cultural organization. The city thus functions as a carnival within a carnival, focused on carnality and depicted through costumes, performances, and the spectacles of buffoonery and sex. But the carnival environment abroad is continuous, and the specific carnival time of Mardi Gras is notable by its absence in this version of New Orleans in the 1930s. Algren's descriptions are steadfastly those of a paganized world without end.

Detailed as a hellish environment, New Orleans—and, in particular, Perdido Street, where the prostitutes, peep shows, and freak shows are located—is structured by the Janus-faced requirements of the city's white interest groups as a land of fantasies but also as one of moral instruction. The red-light district is owned by "stuffed shirts and do-righties" (WWS, 104), who, on a Sunday, hypocritically attend their churches to hear the preacher denounce the activities of the prostitutes. Indeed, women are as much the focus of moral attacks as they are the victims of physical ones at the hands of men in this novel. The displacement of social guilt and responsibility onto the females expunges the hegemonic males of their exploitative involvement in the sex and display subculture of the town. Fenced off as a separate area of physicality and degraded Otherness, Perdido Street is a space of visual sexuality operated by the desires of the white male gaze. It is a region of displacement and pay-per-view entertainment, of sex shows, and of Others on display.

New Orleans as representative of the United States in 1931 is highlighted by Algren's descriptions of the inversions of American reality due to the Depression. A "backward swing of the moral pendulum" (WWS, 113) leads to excesses across the American nation with the rise of gangster activity during the last years of Prohibition. Moreover, "[t]he Ladder of Success had been inverted, the top was the bottom, the bottom was the top. Leaders of men still sporting gold watches were lugging baby photographs door-to-door with their soles flapping. Physicians were out selling skin lighteners, and ship captains queued in hope of a cabin boy's mop and pail" (WWS, 113). Into this world turned upside down Dove arrives, starting his new life as a door-to-door coffeepot salesman in the American South's carnival town. His early adventures in New Orleans revolve around a string of sexual encounters with black women or with prostitutes. Inevitably, he comes into contact with the pimp, Finnerty, who temporarily employs him to deflower girls he intends to use as prostitutes. After a brief involvement with this enterprise and a short apprenticeship with Rhino Gross, a maker of contraceptives, Dove returns to Finnerty's brothel to perform in a peep-show act that extends his former role as a titular "deflowerer" of "virgins," a contrived exhibition of repeated fake performances of the male fantasies of the paying viewers. Located next to Dockery's bar, the entrance to this sexual world is framed in theatrics and is populated by former actors and outcasts of America's traveling carnivals.

Doc Dockery's is a place where time is held in stasis. Fitted out in the trappings of the America before the crash of 1929, this is an illegal speakeasy that negates the contingent reality of Prohibition beyond its doors. The regulars here are "theater people who had lost their theater: ingénues, leading men, stagehands, ticket brokers, managers of road shows, starlets and prima donnas" (WWS, 154). These disenfranchised performers congregate in a theatricalized space that, on occasion, provides violent spectacles for their entertainment. The monstrosity of such occasions is sealed off from view: the doors and shutters are closed over as the men battle for dominance and position within this degraded and carnivalized world. Dockery's is its own lawless realm; no police ever enter the building, and consequently, the justices and punishments meted out in this location are subject only to the opinions of the gathered spectators. Thus, the crownings and uncrownings that pattern the routines of Dockery's bar double as the carnival events of Bakhtinian readings and of American variations on the theme: the participation of the crowd is essential, but the eventual judgments are as irreversible as they are physically realized.

This New Orleans speakeasy is a place out of time and an arena of competition between the various carnivalized individuals. Clearly manifested in the fight between Schmidt and Dove Linkhorn, Dockery's becomes an enclosed zone of opposition and confrontation in which the displaced identities of pimps, peep-show performers, freaks, and prostitutes interact or observe the violence that underwrites the relationships in the text. The disconnection between each of the characters—whether familial, social, or sexual—is the predominant feature of the relationships in Algren's carnivalized universe. That universe is situated and realized primarily in New Orleans in this narrative but is, by extension, manifested throughout the Depression era United States of the 1930s.

Despite the loss of his legs, Schmidt dominates the interactions within Dockery's bar. A powerful man, born in a carny and once the strong man billed (ironically, given his later injuries) as "ACHILLES THE BIRMINGHAM STRONG BOY" (WWS, 255), he has a deformity that has decreased neither his sexual nor his violent appetites. He is a physically distorted individual who has "lived among human skeletons, 500-pound women, dog-faced boys, spider men, living heads, geeks, half-men-half-women and dwarfs in the maimed world of sideshow exhibitions" (WWS, 239). Although he had been humiliated as a freak exhibit known as "The Living Half," in which he was required to sit on "his home-made platform in the freakish sun, looking down at the farmers in town to see the freaks" (WWS, 257), his shame is now forgotten by "the lost and the damned of Perdido Street" (WWS, 258). His one interest is his relationship with the prostitute Hallie, a black woman who appears to be white. Echoing Twain's portrayal of Roxy in *Pudd'nhead Wilson* (1894), Hallie's dual identity is itself a freakish category within American society. Hallie's ability to pass as white enables her to earn a living in a trade restricted in this region to white women. Her racial "disguise" is figured in reverse when she and Dove, who have run away together from New Orleans, watch a performance of *Othello* in which the lead actor has "a bad job of makeup" (WWS, 269). The theatricalization of race that this dramatic spectacle signifies is also symbolically twinned with the revenge plot of Shakespeare's play, acted out in Algren's text by Schmidt's beating of Dove, a confrontation motivated by the latter's liaison with Hallie and by his performances as Big Stingaree, which fill Schmidt with disgust. The climax of the sexual politics in the novel is this "staged" fight between its two most overtly sexual men, both of them "carnival" performers at one time or another and both of whom are uncrowned at the conclusion of the fight.

On leaving Arroyo, Dove's character mutates and evolves to fit his changing environments. Whether nicknamed Red by Kitty, or costumed in a garish white suit with yellow shoes, or perceived to be an "ungodly clown" (WWS, 237) by Schmidt because of his Stingaree outfit of a black bandana, red or yellow shirt, and cowboy boots, Dove is constantly performing throughout the novel. Even when jailed in a racially segregated prison, he is suspected of being "Injun" (WWS, 311). In conjunction with the other performing identities in the text, Dove is entered into a carnivalization of human physicality and sexuality that functions as a depraved spectacle stripped of its reproductive potential. A city "full of lonesome monsters" (WWS, 207)—signaled, for instance, by the naval lieutenant's wish to be scolded by a "black mammy" figure—New Orleans is a space of fantasy and degradation realized in grotesque displays of sex, race, and physical disability. Dove's manipulation of a clownish greenhorn act marks him as a disruptive figure in this landscape. He capitalizes on each of the connections he makes throughout the narrative; for example, unlike Kitty, he escapes arrest after their shop robbery; he switches Finnerty's one hundred dollars for ten dollars to dupe both him and a gullible prostitute; and he steals Gross's hoarded savings. Either as the subversive Red or as the ludicrous Stingaree, Dove is incorporated within highly color-coded environments. If he functions as a new incarnation of aspects of Twain's *The Adventures of Huckleberry Finn*, then it is as a 1930s amalgamation of Twain's characters the King and the Duke, all three of them conmen focused entirely on their own advancement.

Algren's specification that the years 1930 to 1932, in which the action of this novel occurs, are ones of inversions and disorder would suggest that the events take place within a carnival time out of time, thus fulfilling one aspect of Bakhtinian theory. Indeed, Algren also makes clear that with Prohibition in its last phase, this is a liminal period within United States history disconnected from regular social processes and standing between alternate forms of cultural control and social legislation. Yet the reversal of time in Arroyo and the dislocation of New Orleans from any sense of contemporary time indicate by extrapolation that the United States is continually functioning within a suspended or altered reality. As Algren notes, the whole of America, as well as its economic and social structures, has been inverted by Prohibition and in the wake of the Wall Street crash; such reversals, mapping in some respects Bakhtin's delineations of the carnivalesque, are based on a new and alternative version of the grotesque.

There is no redemptive laughter in these carnivalized and grotesque landscapes peopled by former carnival hands, abnormal identities, and disfigured individuals. Further, the carnival(ized) districts of New Orleans are not disconnected from the rest of the city; they are integral parts of its functioning and are controlled by white hegemonic forces of social power and cultural conditioning. American carnival, or the carnivalizing impulse within America in the 1930s of *A Walk on the Wild Side*, is one that is exploitive of the opportunities of the Depression era at a time when economic and political forces have become destabilized or even inverted. The carnival reality of F. Scott Fitzgerald's *The Great Gatsby* (1925)—in which anything can happen in the northeastern state locations of Manhattan and of East and West Egg, Long Island—has become, in the New Orleans of this text, one in which the processes and entertainments of American society are, at least at the visible level, in the hands of pimps, panhandlers, carnival hands, and prostitutes who provide staged performances of sexuality and fantasy. At a further remove, the white fathers, Algren's "Daddy" figures, are those that manipulate the "reality" of these carnivalized locations. Indeed, these spaces, filled with carnival hands and theatrical and sexual performers, have replaced the nation's temporary or traveling versions of carnival. New Orleans is American culture made manifest: the inversion of social hierarchies, the carnivalization of seeing, and the monetarization of human interaction by way of brothels and prostitution are, for Algren, the United States in microcosm.

Algren focuses on the normally unseen and the typically displaced. Spectacle and seeing are of the utmost importance in this text: Dove loses his vision after the fight with Schmidt, disfigured by a man who himself has been disfigured; further, there is a concentration on disguise and costuming, particularly in the case of Dove (and his various namings) but also of Hallie, whose "whiteness" is actually a matter of theatrics and concealment; once again, race, entered into a theatrics of American identity, has been carnivalized and placed on display. Dove operates in a landscape of fairy tale—in a land that wishes to make the make-believe real and that needs to do so in order to alleviate the depressed reality of the time. Even Fitz's weekly sermons in the backwater of Arroyo raise a crowd of spectators hoping for light relief from their own troubles. The boundary between reality and fantasy has been problematized within this American landscape, and Algren's focus is on the characters who populate the territories of carnival and of carnivalized reality. Each person encountered is involved within an economy of vision that is based on carnival representations of identity.

In a society out of kilter as a result of the dual disturbances of Prohibition and the Depression and in the American city traditionally associated with carnival rituals, Algren plots a novel that stages tensions between alternative forms of carnival. In conjunction with his lead character, Algren is successful as a disrupter of social and cultural norms: "[Dove's] rise to the top in a profession which society regards as the bottom is significant, since the transformation of conventional scales of value in this book is one of Algren's signal contributions to the development of the modern American novel."[13] *A Walk on the Wild Side* places American carnival in alternate spheres, and the New Orleans depicted is the overt manifestation of a covert impulse within 1930s American culture. American society is carnivalized and inverted; the "regular" routines and orders have ceased as a result of the Depression; American social patterns have been reorganized by the postwar measures of Prohibition and female emancipation; and familial bonds are severed in Algren's loveless territories of distortion and displacement. Participation and spectation become problematic concerns in a realm in which power and authority have been systematically confused. Algren does employ aspects of the carnivalesque as outlined by Bakhtin, particularly in relation to the popular festive forms of crowning and uncrowning: "In such a system the king is the clown. He is elected by all the people and is mocked by all the people. He is abused and beaten when the time of his reign is over, just as the carnival dummy of winter or of the dying year is mocked, beaten, torn to pieces, burned, or drowned even in our time."[14] Dove's clowning is not allowed to last, just as Schmidt's physical dominance must be reeled in by the democratic arbitrations of the spectators. Positions of ascendancy are not maintained. The fight is a set piece of this particular carnival world of New Orleans and occurs as another in a line of brutal conflicts in this zone of violence and power. Closer in its deployment of a carnivalesque associated with European traditions—such as Mardi Gras—this is an American space that accommodates patterns of carnival ritual, bodily debasement, and degraded sexuality contiguous with American versions of carnival and the grotesque:

exhibited spectacles of deformity, "freaks" born or made, blackness as a facial disguise rather than a racial category. For the crownings and uncrownings of Bakhtinian carnival, the novel does have two temporary kings—Dove and Schmidt—both of them ascendant and both of them debunked by the democratic impulses of the spectating crowd. Indeed, it is once the crowd enters the combative action that an alteration of the carnival register occurs, transfiguring the accustomed spectation with American carnival into the active participation of European rituals of carnival uncrowning. Algren provides a textual site for the satisfaction of both carnival impulses in *A Walk on the Wild Side*: Dockery's bar is the ultimate manifestation of that dual impulse in the text, the site of staged spectacles of freakishness and monstrosity and, alternatively, a stage for the fulfillment of the egalitarian and democratic impulses of Bakhtinian carnival forms.

Notes

1. Nelson Algren, quoted in H. E. F. Donohue, *Conversations with Nelson Algren* (New York: Hill & Wang, 1964), 49.

2. James R. Giles, *Confronting the Horror: The Novels of Nelson Algren* (Kent, Ohio: Kent State University Press, 1989), 74.

3. I provide a fuller account of the term *American carnival* and its operations in a range of nineteenth- and twentieth-century American texts and contexts in Philip McGowan, *American Carnival: Seeing and Reading American Culture* (Westport, Conn.: Greenwood Press, 2001).

4. For more in-depth examinations of this area, see Toni Morrison, *Playing in the Dark: Whiteness and the American Literary Imagination* (London: Picador, 1993); Valerie Babb, *Whiteness Visible: The Meaning of Whiteness in American Literature and Culture* (New York: New York University Press, 1998); and *Whiteness: A Critical Reader*, ed. Mike Hill (New York: New York University Press, 1997).

5. I am referring in particular here to the newspaper competition run by the Hearst publishing empire in 1929 to find a replacement for national Prohibition. More than seventy thousand people entered this competition in the four months that it ran (January to April 1929). For a fuller account of the more-carnivalized suggestions of alcohol control and civil punishment, see McGowan, *American Carnival* and *Temperance—or Prohibition? The Hearst Temperance Contest Committee*, ed. Francis J. Tietsort (New York: J. J. Little & Ives, 1929).

6. Bill Brown, *The Material Unconscious: American Amusement, Stephen Crane, and the Economies of Play* (Cambridge, Mass.: Harvard University Press, 1996), 212.

7. Georges Bataille, "The Deviations of Nature," 53–56, in *Visions of Excess: Selected Writings, 1927–1939*, edited and with an introduction by Allan Stoekl (Minneapolis: University of Minnesota Press, 1985), 55.

8. Peter Stallybrass and Allon White, *The Politics and Poetics of Transgression* (London: Methuen, 1986), 110.

9. Mikhail Bakhtin, *Rabelais and His World*, trans. Hélène Iswolsky (Bloomington: Indiana University Press, 1984), 7. Moreover, as he notes in *Problems of Dostoyevsky's Poetics*, "In carnival everyone is an active participant, everyone communes in the carnival act. Carnival is not contemplated, and, strictly speaking, not even performed." Mikhail Bakhtin, *Problems of Dostoevsky's Poetics*, ed. and trans. Caryl Emerson (Minneapolis: University of Minnesota Press, 1984), 122.

10. I am indebted to my colleague Josh Cohen from Goldsmiths College, University of London, for this use of the phrase a "politics of seeing" borrowed from his discussions of postmodern U.S. fiction in his book *Spectacular Allegories: Postmodern American Writing and the Politics of Seeing* (London: Pluto Press, 1998). Cohen's rescuing of the visual from Jean Baudrillard's nonmaterial realm of simulation and reproducibility parallels my arguments here with regard to American carnival: the visual/visualization of identity (race/ethnic/Other) in American carnival is specifically embedded within, and a result of, material processes of politicized organization and the hegemonics of monological American social constructions.

11. Nelson Algren, *A Walk on the Wild Side* (1956; repr., Edinburgh, Scotland: Rebel, 1999), 17. Further references are to this edition and are cited parenthetically as WWS.

12. Bakhtin, *Rabelais and His World*, 194.

13. Martha Heasley Cox and Wayne Chatterton, *Nelson Algren* (Boston: Twayne, 1975), 76.

14. Bakhtin, *Rabelais and His World*, 197.

"It Was Dope!": The Paperback Revolution and the Literary Reputation of Nelson Algren

Bill Savage

A GRAPHIC REPRESENTATION OF NELSON ALGREN'S LITERARY REPUTATION would resemble a roller coaster. Algren began to write and build a solid name for himself in the context of the socially and politically engaged literary tradition of the Depression; in the decade after World War II, Algren was widely considered an up-and-coming novelist at the center of American literature, praised by Ernest Hemingway as better than William Faulkner. After devastating critical attacks on his 1956 novel *A Walk on the Wild Side*, Algren was unable to get an advance to write a novel, and his stock plummeted. By the middle of the 1970s, he was largely forgotten; at the time of his death in 1981, all of his work was out of print. But since the late 1980s, almost all of Algren's work has again become available, dramas based on his work and life are being produced, and he is getting more scholarly and critical attention than he had at any time during his life.

Any understanding of Algren's literary reputation must take into account transformations that took place in American literary culture in the middle of his career in terms of both the role of politics in literature and material aspects of literary production and consumption. In the first, successful, half of Algren's career, political content in a novel did not disqualify it from consideration as serious literature. General readers—and their professional counterparts, critics and reviewers—judged books on both form and content, on what a writer had to say, and on how well the writer said it. But cold war politics eliminated that balanced approach to literature; to the formalist scholars who rose to prominence in the 1950s and effectively ended Algren's career as a novelist, any leftist political content sufficed as a pretext to dismiss a book out of hand. Literary criticism written in this mode proceeded from the suspect assumption that great literature transcends the limitations of politics, history, sociology, culture, and time. Hence, fiction like Algren's that addressed social concerns of very specific places and times could not be considered candidates for greatness, eventual canonical status. That shift in literary values has been characterized by its proponents as a triumph of aesthetics over ideology, a pursuit of universal human truth. In reality, as Barbara Herrnstein Smith has argued, when critics claim to look for aesthetics alone and ignore the political content of art, they actually endorse the status quo by default.[1] But claiming to be apolitical, to attend to truth and beauty, sweetness and light, was a strategy that made eminent sense for scholars and academic critics in 1950s America. In an atmosphere of nuclear paranoia, McCarthyism and the House Un-American Activities Committee, loyalty oaths for teachers, and blacklists in publishing and Hollywood, it was simply safer for one's career to avoid politics. We should not be surprised that the newly powerful academic critics dismissed Algren, along with writers of the 1920s, 1930s, and 1940s such as Jack Conroy, Eskrine Caldwell, and James T. Farrell.

While the evolution of canon making and literary values has been the focus of much theory and criticism written in the past few decades, scholars of canon formation have not sufficiently examined how judgments by literary professionals are communicated to the wider world of readers. The second transformation in American literary culture that influenced the fate of Algren's reputation has been studied primarily by cultural historians, rather than by literary theorists and critics: the rise of the paperback, the paperback revolution. By examining this radical change in the cultural landscape, we can discover a great deal about how literary reputations are made and unmade and communicated to readers both at a given time and in other decades. From the 1939 debut of Pocket Books in the United States onward, paperbacks—both reprints of hardcover novels and original material—made fiction available to millions of new readers. As the New American Library slogan put it, paperbacks provided "Good Reading for the Millions."[2] Whether that shift was a good thing or not depends on your perspective: one person's democratization is another person's dumbing down, but no one can deny that paperbacks utterly transformed the business of bookselling and American literary culture. Books, once published only in expensive hardcover and sold at a few rarified locations, were now for sale seemingly everywhere at prices anyone could afford.

From an elite perspective, the term *paperback original* soon replaced *pulp* as shorthand for lowbrow sensationalistic fiction—the stuff an educated person would not be caught dead reading. That negative association with the pulps makes sense in terms of material culture, because paperbacks were distributed primarily in locations where they had to compete with the pulps for impulse purchases by people who generally did not buy books. Paperback publishers soon began designing lurid packages that would draw the browser's eye away from other distractions at the drugstore, the five-and-dime, or the train station newsstand, and the cover art and design of the paperback began to represent this new form in the public mind. As the paperback historian Thomas L. Bonn stated, "[T]he key aspect of the paperback package, the cover design, symbolizes for reader, writer, and publisher the mass market paperback book industry as a whole."[3] Yet whether approaching literature from a traditional, formalist, conservative position or from the linguistically and ideologically informed angle taken by many poststructuralist thinkers, the paperback as a cultural form seems off the point, contingent, a mere artifact of commercial culture rather than a central characteristic of the production and communication of literary values. Literary scholars overlook the influence of paperback cover design on readers in part because as historians of paperback design themselves admit, "The cover . . . really is an advertising tool" and hence beneath notice.[4] This blind spot results, I believe, from the fact that academics often unreflectively talk about "texts," often as though they existed in some platonic ether, above and beyond material concerns.

We forget at our peril, though, the fact that readers in the world beyond the walls of the groves of academe do not read *texts*: they read *books*. The material properties of particular editions of books—the overt textual content of blurbs and other jacket copy, the implicit semiotics of cover design, the cultural significance inherent in materials used in manufacture, the literary values enacted in methods of buying and selling—communicate a writer's literary reputation to readers outside the literary establishment. Scholars usually, and correctly, address Algren's 1950s era decanonization in the context of the rise of academic, formalist literary criticism and the corresponding devaluation of politically engaged literature. But we can best understand the roller coaster of Algren's reputation—both his decanonization and his current revival—by examining the way he has been packaged and sold: the material manifestation of literary reputation.

Furthermore, to connect the question of Algren's reputation to a larger discourse, aspects of material literary culture can help untie an old philosophical knot: the hermeneutic circle. Interpretive theorists have long held that readers can understand a part of a text only with a sense of what the whole text means, yet the meaning of a whole text is composed of the meaning of its parts. The problem of genre placement—a sense of what the text at hand is and how to approach it properly—is at the heart of the matter, whichever school of interpretive theory one subscribes to. The conservative, authorially oriented theorist E. D. Hirsch Jr. asserts that every text's meaning is based on its "intrinsic genre."[5] The social constructionist theorist Stanley Fish bases his arguments about the power of interpretive communities on the issue of genre. Middle-of-the-road theorists such as Peter J. Rabinowitz, who combine both an authorial and a reader-response perspective, also rely on genre as a starting point for readers' interpretive behavior. But none of those theorists addresses adequately the question of *how* readers get a sense of a text's genre. Hirsch claims we simply make an educated guess at intrinsic genre, "that sense of the whole by means of which an interpreter can correctly understand any part of its determinacy."[6] In other words, we enter the hermeneutic circle by guesswork, but Hirsch does not address what readers might base their guess on. Fish's arguments almost always elide his own participation in pointing his audience toward a generic beginning.[7] Rabinowitz claims that readers' initial stance toward a book is based on "an intuitive mix of experience and faith, knowledge and hunch—plus a certain amount of luck,"[8] but he too fails to consider explicitly what goes into that intuitive mix, how readers in the world know what sort of break they are about to crack the spine of. A sophisticated understanding of the interpretive consequences of a book's materiality—how it is packaged, bought, and sold—can resolve the problem of the hermeneutic circle, at least for postwar narrative fiction, and can illuminate the evolution of Algren's reputation.

Before readers begin interpreting a text—reading a book—they encounter what I call the *preinterpretive field*: an array of prior readings and evaluations of that text that enables the very act of interpretation by situating the book within commonly understood systems of genre and levels of canonicity. Prior to interpretation of the first word of a text, the material form of the book implicitly and explicitly communicates generic and canonical status: what sort of book it is and how good it is compared with other such books. Thus, with a sense of what the whole means, genre does limit what sort of meaning a text might have: readers have grounds to interpret the individual parts of the book as they move through the overall narrative.

The process is neither simple nor unconflicted, of course; that is why I use the metaphor of a field of possible preinterpretations rather than a linear or obligatory series. It is possible for a reader to pick up a book without encountering any particular interpretation of that text, but it is almost impossible to conceive of a reader starting a book without encountering some preinterpretation of it. At the very least, the reader would know that some literary professionals in the publishing industry thought the book worthwhile; the reader would also have a sense of a book's genre based on where the bookseller shelved it; and its relative canonical value would be communicated by material form, size, cost, weight of paper, and cover design. As Mary Louise Pratt puts it, "[T]he tangible physical features that distinguish pamphlets, newspapers, magazines, journals and books express (in a code which must be learned) a wide variety of differences in intended function, intended Audience [*sic*], stringency of selection, range of subject matter, and so on."[9]

Perhaps the most important distinction communicated by the material form of a book—and the one that most influenced the way many readers understood Algren's canonical status—is the distinction between serious and popular genres. That distinction is of course a messy and socially constructed one—one that postmodern and poststructuralist theories further complicate. But for the nonacademic reader in the world, it is fairly straightforward: some books you read in school; some you read at the beach. Rabinowitz has analyzed at some length the relationship between elite, or academic, reading and popular reading, and for the consideration of Algren's career, the main thing to keep in mind is this: the distinction between serious texts and popular texts is fundamentally a genre distinction that structures the interpretive behavior of readers. We read books in what Rabinowitz calls "intertextual grids": that is, we read books with other books like them in mind, as a basis of comparison.[10] Readers transform serious and popular texts differently: in general, we read serious texts for thematic and philosophical concerns. We read popular texts for the satisfactions afforded by the well-worked-out plot—be it a romance, a western, or a detective novel. That generalization does not mean that serious books lack plot or that thrillers do not have themes; it is a matter of relative emphasis related to what aspects of the texts readers attended to and how they judge a text's success. A serious book with no serious theme is a failure, as is a thriller with no thrills.

A writer's or a book's position in the serious/popular spectrum is reproduced—and for readers unfamiliar with a particular author or book, produced in the first place—by the material form of the particular edition of any book. The issue for Algren and his literary reputation is his position at the conjunction of two major shifts in American literary culture. Just as he was being dismissed as not serious by formalist, right-wing canon makers, he was also packaged and sold to general readers as a writer of various popular genres: the lurid urban exposé, the drug abuse morality tale, or the juvenile delinquent novel. In one of the more potent attacks on Algren's 1956 novel *A Walk on the Wild Side*, Leslie A. Fiedler writes that Algren was "a museum piece—the Last of the Proletarian Writers. . . . It is, then, as an exotic, a romantic purveyor of escape literature that Algren must be read—this apparent 'realist' whose fictional world is at the ultimate remove from any reality his readers know."[11] The material form of Algren's books echoed the critical dismissal of him as a mere "purveyor of escape literature," and for readers outside the academy, Algren's packaging, especially the covers of various paperback editions of his fiction, created and perpetuated his noncanonical status. Of course, that argument runs counter to the adage that you cannot judge a book by its cover. I would respond in two ways: First, readers obviously do judge books by their cover, both figuratively by equating surface and depth and literally by having their interpretive behavior influenced by book covers. Our culture would not need a warning against that behavior if it were not commonplace: you only have to say, "Don't count your chickens before they're hatched," if people actually do make plans based on uncertain future contingencies. (Interestingly, Fiedler actually discusses Art Shay's dust jacket photo of *A Walk on the Wild Side*, comparing the picture of Algren in a shadowy, garbage-strewn back alley to well-known photos of Hemingway on safari and Faulkner in front of an antebellum mansion. Fiedler's comment simultaneously shows the high standing that Algren had at the time—since being compared, even negatively, to Hemingway and Faulkner implies status—and suggests that even professional readers attend to packaging.) Second, the commercial aspect of publishing must be kept in mind: buyers choose to purchase not *texts* but particular *books* and particular sorts of *books*. Publishers have an economic incentive to deliver the goods and to make those goods readily identifiable to customers. As James B. Twitchell describes the process, "Whoever said you can't judge a book by its cover did not understand paperback publishing. You *must* be able to judge content by cover, and especially in category fiction, by the background alone. . . . [Illustrators have created] a grammar of cover art every bit as sophisticated as most of the internal texts.[12] For writers like Algren, whose status as a writer was promising but in flux—what Richard Ohmann has described as "precanonical"[13]—and whose texts are subject to misinterpretation or generic misplacement, the influence of cover art on book buyers and readers cannot be overestimated.

To understand fully the effect of the ways Algren was packaged and sold on his literary reputation, I need to historicize the production of his literary reputation and how his books were packaged in relation to books by other authors. The earliest American paperbacks, such as the 1939 Pocket Books editions of Emily Brontë's *Wuthering Heights* and James Hilton's *Lost Horizon*, had sedate cover art that resembled the dust jackets of hardcover books (images of covers discussed here are available online at www.billsavagebooks.com). But paperback publishers soon learned that since they were competing for impulse purchases at the newsstand, they had to have eye-catching covers that would stand out and compete with lurid pulp magazines rather than hardcovers in bookstores. Pulps had long emphasized sex and violence, and paperbacks followed suit, relying on cover art that emphasized plot and used a "brooding realism to which a thick veneer of sex and sadism was imposed" to attract the potential buyer.[14] That relative emphasis mirrors our understanding of the difference between serious and popular genres themselves. A scene from the plot marks a book as popular; the more abstract, figurative, or typographic a book's cover, the more serious it is. Then as now, sex sells, and so long-forgotten books such as H. E. Bates's *The Nature of Love* (1953) and Albert Moravia's *Conjugal Love* (1952) featured suggestive bedroom scenes in order to sell as many books as possible. Some publishers, naturally, went even further, designing lurid, violent, and hypersexualized covers that became something of an industry norm, although the racialized sadism of such books as Roy Flannagan's *The Whipping* (1950, which featured hooded Klansmen barging into the bedroom of a scantily clad woman) and James Hadley Chase's *12 Chinks and a Woman* (1952, showing three Asian men beating and binding a white woman, over the prone body of a white man) are admittedly extreme examples.

As is so often the case in American culture, the new form caused grave concern over a potential threat to the morals of young and impressionable readers, and congressional hearings on paperback cover design were actually held. As Bonn has put it: "Throughout the late 1940s and early 1950s paperback books were attacked by censoring agencies, both official and unofficial, that sought to purge the wire racks of lurid literature. This period of lost esteem for Pocket Books and other paperback houses has been described as a time of 'sex, sensationalism, and statutory rape.' "[15] Paperback cover illustrations from this era have lately acquired a pop culture cachet, as posters, postcards, and T-shirts reproduce these images with a certain nostalgic air: ah, the good old days of lurid paperbacks. Coffee-table books have been published examining those paperbacks and pulps as hip retro collectibles.[16] But this unreflective embrace of the paperback illustration helps hide the real consequences of the material aspects of literary culture on readers and on the reputations of writers such as Algren who, just at the moment when their long-term canonical status was subject to debate, were packaged and sold as trash.

We also forget that publishers did not just package little-known and new writers that way: they also sold canonical authors such as Hemingway and Faulkner in packages that now seem totally inappropriate. The 1949 edition of *The Sun Also Rises* features the blurb "Could he live without the power to love?"; the 1951 edition of *Pylon* resembles nothing so much as a crime thriller. Most publishers made no distinction between serious and popular texts: covers were designed to sell as many books as possible, and if that meant emphasizing the one scene in the novel that can be read as sexual or excuse some innuendo, so be it. Publishers defended the practice, claiming that such covers "attracted a new and broader readership which otherwise would not have been led to this fine literature."[17] Another publisher, though, was more honest: "[T]he only good cover art is the one that brings the twenty-five cents across the counter."[18] Hemingway and Faulkner had literary reputations that could easily withstand a certain amount of generic misplacement or misemphasis, but Algren did not.

The relationship that the semiotics of paperback cover illustration posits between the potential buyer/reader and the subject matter of the novel is fundamental to the construction of literary reputations. Many of the early paperbacks construct their potential buyer as a voyeur, someone sneaking a look into a world he or she otherwise would never enter. The early paperback cover that set the tone for much of the rest of the industry was the 1946 Signet edition of Erskine Caldwell's *God's Little Acre*, which featured a wooden fence and a knothole through which the reader peers at the shack beyond. While Caldwell was a serious and politically engaged writer attempting to depict the brutalizing consequences of the poverty of much of the rural South, the paperback editions of his novels, along with their dramatic adaptations on stage and in film, have made him out to be someone interested primarily in giving his readers voyeuristic glimpses of rural ignorance, debauchery, sex, incest, and violence. The cover of a later Caldwell paperback, *A Woman in the House* (1949), makes this metaphoric voyeurism almost literal, as it takes the peephole metaphor at its word and shows a half-clad young woman, in bed, through a keyhole rendered with total realism, right down to the screws on the lock plate that holds the doorknob in place. Paperback cover design made readers into voyeurs.

Soon enough, though, publishers, artists, and book designers began the process that eventually led to the current split between mass-market and trade paperbacks, and between disreputable and respectable designs. The fact that now paperbacks can be perfectly respectable explains in part why finding writers such as Hemingway and Faulkner packaged trashily is something of a shock to contemporary readers. But even as early as 1947, designers began to aestheticize the voyeurism of the knothole design, making it more figurative and therefore potentially serious, as we see in editions of Caldwell's *Tragic Ground* (1948) and Faulkner's *Sanctuary* (1947). On the cover of *Tragic Ground*, the knothole has been transformed into a torn sheet with the image of woman on it; in *Sanctuary*, it is a photo that has been ripped up and pinned back together. Both images still emphasize the female form and metaphorically make the reader a voyeur but do so in a way that requires interpretation by the reader, just as a serious text would—and much more subtly than *A Woman in the House* or *God's Little Acre*. Whether explicitly serious or implicitly voyeuristic, the illustrations on the covers of paperbacks would provide readers with an interpretive starting point, a preinterpretive assumption about the generic and canonical status of the book at hand.

When we recall, as such theorists as Jane P. Tompkins have so thoroughly demonstrated,[19] that canons shift over time, we can also trace the evolution of an author's canonical status by looking at the changes in the packaging of the author's books. This phenomenon is perhaps best demonstrated by various editions of Raymond Chandler's 1939 novel *The Big Sleep*. The 1950 Pocket Books edition depicts the moment when the detective Philip Marlowe discovers Carmen Sternwood, the daughter of his client, drugged, nude, and sitting above the dead body of the pornographer and blackmailer A. G. Geiger. The blurb reads, "Philip Marlowe knew this luscious mantrap had been a witness to MURDER." Such emphasis on plot clearly marks the text as a popular detective novel, because of the emphasis placed on plot by popular genres and expected from such books by readers of those genres. The 1958 edition demonstrates the fact that designers use earlier covers as the basis for new ones: the blurb now reads, "A luscious mantrap leads Philip Marlowe to a West Coast murder wave" as the too-good-to-pass-up phrase "luscious mantrap" remains. This illustration depicts another key scene in the plot—when Marlowe returns home to find Carmen waiting in his bed—but this moment by itself is not enough, and the illustrator makes conditions even more extreme by giving Carmen a gun. In the novel, while Carmen tries to seduce Marlowe, she is not armed. Both illustrations situate the presumably male potential buyer in a position to stare at Carmen's body, another subtle form of voyeurism that places the novel in the realm of popular rather than serious texts.

When Raymond Chandler's critical reputation as one of the founders of the American hard-boiled detective novel begins to grow, his stature is both *reflected in and created by* material aspects of *The Big Sleep*. Literary professionals, aware of the growing scholarly attention paid Chandler, reflect Chandler's new reputation in their work, packaging him in ways that mark him as a serious writer. For readers unfamiliar with his novels, these designs create that reputation, informing them of his status. The 1972 Ballantine edition of *The Big Sleep* has a stylized cover—featuring a woman's face, transfixed perhaps in ecstasy, amidst a luxuriant array of orchids and Venus flytraps. Such a stylized image, as does any serious text, requires readerly interpretation. The sexual imagery of earlier editions lingers, but it does not depict a moment from the plot: it depicts an image to be considered and interpreted thematically (there are, for instance, orchids but no Venus flytraps in the text of the novel, but these carnivorous plants aptly symbolize the dangerous Sternwood sisters). The first trade paperback edition (1988) sends a mixed message: while the higher-price, larger-size, heavier paper, and sophisticated cover photo all tell a reader that this is a serious text, the image itself is plot-oriented. The cover photo depicts a moment just before that pictured on the first paperback, as Geiger takes a photo of Carmen, but the arty, soft-focus black-and-white image pushes the novel toward the serious. The second trade paperback edition (1992) marks the novel as almost completely serious. Its illustration, a car being driven over a bridge, could be a cover for any number of novels and depicts nothing from the plot at all. Finally, Chandler completes his migration into the canon with the Library of America edition, featuring a serious black-and-white author's photo, hard covers, acid-free paper, and highbrow design that firmly place Chandler in an acknowledged body of serious literature.

We can trace the history of Algren's critical reception and literary reputation by examining how his texts were packaged and sold to readers unfamiliar with his fiction. Algren's work was dismissed by various right-wing canon makers as beneath the consideration of the serious reader: not just bad, but not worth arguing about—merely popular fiction—and the early paperback editions of his work provided nothing to contradict that critical dismissal. While the first hardcover edition of *The Man with the Golden Arm* (1949) featured a needle, its primarily typographic and figurative design (a needle among the symbols of different suits of playing cards) marks the book as serious. The first paperback edition (1951) also evokes serious literary status, as it quotes the *Time* magazine review of the novel at length. Yet the status of the novel begins to change almost immediately: on the second paperback edition, published the same year, a cover begins the association of this novel with junkie fiction. Purportedly a scene from the plot, the grimly realistic painting depicts Frankie Machine with his morphine paraphernalia, about to shoot up despite the concerned attention of the woman on the bed with him. No such scene ever takes place in the novel, but as Bonn pointed out, cover artists rarely had time to read all of the novels they were illustrating.[20] Such an image—along with the shrill blurb "More powerful than a woman's love . . . more binding than a man's word. . . . *It was DOPE!*"—marks the text, for the reader unfamiliar with it, as a shocker, subgenre junkie novel, a popular genre read primarily for the illicit thrill of touring the urban underworld of drugs.

Nothing could be further from the truth about Algren's masterpiece, and at the same time, no generic misplacement is more understandable. In *The Man with the Golden Arm*, Frankie Machine's addiction to morphine serves as an indictment of an American culture that so thoroughly dehumanizes and alienates Frankie that morphine makes sense to him. The novel is not an exposé of a junkie's life along the lines of William S. Burroughs's 1951 potboiler *Junkie* or of tawdry paperbacks like Robert W. Taylor's *The Junk Pusher* (1954) or Richard Deming's *Death of a Pusher* (1964), both of which feature covers drawn in similar styles and similarly lurid blurbs. Those two books could have been on the same newsstand rack as *The Man with the Golden Arm*, and the illustrations and blurbs would have made them almost indistinguishable from each other, at least in terms of genre placement. But the novel's title character *is* a junkie, and his battle with morphine, however symbolic of larger things to a sympathetic reader, can be extricated from Algren's purposes and used to place a book in a popular genre, where it might sell more copies. There is evidence that just such a decision was made at some point: intriguingly, in some copies of this second paperback edition of *The Man with the Golden Arm*, the *"It was DOPE!"* cover is actually a dust jacket glued over the serious first paperback edition. We can infer that a warehouse full of unsold serious novels inspired Pocket Books to add a cover that might sell to another market.

We must remember that a reader unfamiliar with Algren's work would have nothing else with which to classify the text—to assign it to some genre or another—in order to begin the process of interpretation. And just as this design would lead a reader to place *The Man with the Golden Arm* in an intertextual grid with other junkie novels, other books by Algren fit into similar lurid, lowbrow genres. The first Avon editions of *Never Come Morning* (1948) and *The Neon Wilderness* (1952) use sex to sell very directly. *Never Come Morning* features a young woman sitting on a single bed, clad in a nightgown, contemplating her fate; *The Neon Wilderness* features a tall curvaceous blonde on a background of neon bar signs and cityscape. While the cover of *Never Come Morning* depicts a moment from the plot—when Steffi Rostenkowski ponders the chain of events that put her in a brothel—the Mae Westish hooker of *The Neon Wilderness* is pure bookseller's fantasy. No such character appears in any of the stories in this collection, and the montage design evokes urban exposés such as Jack Lait and Lee Mortimer's *Chicago Confidential* (1950). The issue of how cover design associates Algren's work with lowbrow genres is perhaps made most clear in the mid-1950s Avon edition of *Never Come Morning*. A new pop genre of the mid-1950s was the juvenile delinquent, or JD, novel. Written in response to the postwar urban crisis and the perceived rise of teen street gangs, such books pandered to a taste for voyeuristic insight into the supposedly new phenomenon. *Never Come Morning* is described in a blurb as "TEEN-AGE TRAGEDY" The Great Novel of JUVENILE DELINQUENCY," and the illustration shows a young woman on a set of bedsprings in a red-brick urban basement; one man stands above her as she tries to cover her breasts, while two other men come smoking and leering down stairs into the basement, presumably with less-than-honorable intentions. The illustration not only stresses a moment from the plot, it firmly associates Algren's novel with the JD genre. And to a reader unfamiliar with Algren, this serious novel of urban crime and punishment would be virtually indistinguishable from Lenard Kaufman's *Juvenile Delinquents* (n.d., probably 1956). Kaufman's cover features another scantily clad young woman, accepting a cigarette from one young man while two others lean over her, next to garbage cans on the front stoop of a redbrick slum building. The parallels between the cover designs are striking: the use of redbrick and steps (symbolic of urban decay, perhaps, along with the garbage can and bedsprings), the three-boys-to-one-girl ratio, the revealing dress, the cigarettes. Kaufman's novel, originally titled *The Lower Part of the Sky* (retitled as many novels were, to sell more copies to new audiences), may very well be a serious book, too, but to the reader unfamiliar with a writer, the cover provides the initial assumption that allows for interpretation. These covers mark these books as popular rather than serious.

Most important, perhaps, is the way all of these covers—along with later editions of *The Man with the Golden Arm*, which attempt to place the novel in a more serious context—set up a voyeuristic relationship between the reader and Algren's subject matter. As Algren's most perceptive literary critics—Carla Cappetti, Bettina Drew, James R. Giles, James Lewin, and Carlo Rotella—have pointed out in various contexts, Algren's work is dedicated to giving voices to the voiceless and to depicting the real humanity of the people at the bottom of American culture—people all too often overlooked or ignored by readers and writers alike. To do so, Algren set out to make readers sympathize with his characters—not to romanticize or idealize them, but to see them as human beings like them, to identify with our shared human nature. The voyeuristic relationship implicitly created by the ways Algren was packaged and sold has exactly the opposite effect: it makes the reader objectify Algren's characters as Other, as alien to the reader. Such an attitude precisely opposes the dominant trend in the post–World War II academic-canon-formation process. As Ohmann has pointed out, this literary world valued novels that told "stories of people trying to live a decent life in contemporary social settings, people represented as analogous to 'us,' rather than as cases to be examined and understood from a clinical distance, as in an older realistic convention."[21] While Algren did work in this older, realistic convention, one of the distinguishing aspects of his fiction is the way he tries to make his subject matter, the characters he writes about, more than just "cases" to be examined by the middle-class reader.

The Chicago writer who most successfully lived up to Ohmann's description of what the postwar canon makers favored is Saul Bellow. The careers of Algren and Bellow begin in a similar place—both literally and metaphorically—as both come out of the Works Progress Administration's Federal Writers' Project. Algren won the first National Book Award in 1950 for *The Man with the Golden Arm*; four years later, Bellow won for *The Adventures of Augie March* (1953). At one point, both Bellow and Algren were considered serious novelists of similar status, yet the two writers' subsequent careers could hardly have been more different. Bellow won the ultimate credential: the Nobel Prize in Literature, in 1976; by the mid-1970s, all of Algren's novels were out of print and he could not get an advance to write another. While their divergent academic receptions might initially suggest that the two authors had little in common, they were both packaged identically in the heyday of the lurid paperback. The 1955 Popular Library edition of *The Adventures of Augie March* is as lurid as any trashy paperback of the day—or even more so, since it features two different scantily clad women: one on the front cover and another on the back, one blonde and one brunette. Later editions of Bellow's first Chicago novel feature covers that either are wholly typographic or that use historical photos or montage illustrations that mark the text as serious literature. This is not to argue that Bellow is not serious. We must remember, though, that whether or not seriousness is inherent in the authorially intended meaning of the text or is socially constructed by readers operating in an interpretive community, it still must be communicated to the reader unfamiliar with the author, and the material aspects of the book communicate that status.

A comparison between the 1984 Penguin editions of these two novels shows how firmly the two authors' reputations were cemented among literary professionals and how even attempts to package Algren in a more serious way still mark him as less than wholly canonical. The 1984 Penguin edition of *The Adventures of Augie March* features a montage cover full of symbolic images requiring interpretation: a man dressed in a T-shirt with a tuxedo jacket, a bald eagle and several women amid a cityscape, a car, snakes intertwined among playing cards. These images require interpretation, relation to some theme or another. Americanness, good and evil, love and death, the city, social and physical mobility—all are suggested by these images, and together they intimate that the novel itself will require symbolic interpretation of theme. Bellow's stature as an author is manifest in the fact that his name, in white, contrasts more sharply with the cover's dark-blue background than does the title, which is in light blue. This seemingly minor detail implies that *who wrote the book* is more important than *which particular book* it might be and, along with the blurb "Winner of the Nobel Prize for Literature" on the back cover, tells prospective readers that they hold a work of serious literature in their hands.

The 1984 Penguin edition of *The Man with the Golden Arm* also features a figurative cover, with a king of hearts playing card pierced by a hypodermic needle. This suggests themes involving love and power, but still, around the lurid symbolic needle, not so subtly reinforcing the idea that the novel is primarily a junkie book. To the right of Algren's name a blurb reads, "Cardsharps, junkies, cops, and hustlers—the classic novel of the urban jungle," and this furthers the characterization of the subject matter as not serious. Lack of such a blurb on the 1984 *The Adventures of Augie March* means that Bellow's novel is just a novel: it is the norm from which a novel "of" something deviates. And "Cardsharps, junkies, cops, and hustlers" in the "urban jungle" are the stuff of pulp fiction still. Significantly, both of these covers, along with the back cover blurbs that reinforce the messages of the front covers, were designed by the same person: one Neil Stuart. Algren's reputation as a writer of junkie fiction, and the design of earlier editions of the novel, outweighed even a strong attempt to market him as a serious writer.

But things have changed, and Algren is undergoing a renaissance. One sure measure of canonical status is the ratio between the number of books written *by* and *about* an author, and while Algren still has written more books than have been written about him, scholars are beginning to attend to his work in new ways. Just as Algren's novels were back in print in the late 1980s thanks to the independent publisher Daniel Simon, the first full-length study of Algren's fiction—Giles's *Confronting the Horror: The Novels of Nelson Algren* —appeared in 1989, soon after Bettina Drew's critical biography *Nelson Algren: A Life on the Wild Side.* Algren's status in academic intellectual culture has been slowly growing since those groundbreaking efforts, as scholars include his work in studies of broader topics or publish more of his material in new form. Cappetti, in *Writing Chicago: Modernism, Ethnography and the Novel*, examines *Never Come Morning* in relation to the mutually influential work of urban sociologists from the University of Chicago and the novels of Algren, Farrell, and Richard Wright. A collection of Algren's stories set in the Southwest—*The Texas Stories of Nelson Algren* (1995), edited and introduced by Drew—has been published by the University of Texas Press. Seven Stories Press has published *Nonconformity: Writing on Writing* (1996), an essay by Algren on literary culture that had been thought lost. Rotella's *October Cities: The Redevelopment of Urban Literature* looks at *Chicago: City on the Make* (1951) and *The Man with the Golden Arm* as examples of literary expressions that lament the decline of the industrialized urban ethnic neighborhood in the context of the growth of the postwar and postindustrial city. In 1999, *The Man with the Golden Arm: 50th Anniversary Critical Edition* was published, the first critical edition of any Algren work; an annotated *Chicago: City on the Make* followed in 2001. These scholarly editions, as well as the book you now hold in your hands, mark a potential return to canonical status for a writer long and unjustly ignored.

Canon formation is a socially meditated, time-consuming, and complex process. Within what might be called the literary establishment, numerous actions define whether or not a writer or a particular text will be taken seriously. Publishers and editors choose to publish books or reject them and once they are published, to keep them in stock or let them go out of print. Editors choose to review or ignore those same books. Critics, scholars, and students overlook or study certain authors or texts, make judgments, write articles in academic journals, and present papers at symposia and conferences. Professors and teachers select some texts for their syllabi. Yet students of canon making have generally ignored these aspects of material culture, which influence how a writer's literary reputation is communicated to readers beyond or outside the literary establishment. The material form a *text* takes—as a *book*—communicates a writer's literary reputation to such readers by situating the text at a particular place in relation to genre and canonicity, providing a starting point for any reader's interpretation.

Once the process of interpretation begins, of course, any number of possible outcomes can ensue because readers are specific people who have individual tastes and preferences as well as particular relationships to various books, reading styles, and genres. Readers who prefer serious fiction might not bother with Algren at all, because of the genres suggested by his packaging. A reader who knew of Algren from some other source might ignore or think inappropriate the various material preinterpretations that set up Algren as a writer of junkie fiction. But note that such a serious starting point does not invalidate the idea of a preinterpretive field: it merely posits a different assumption about genre and canon at the start of the process of reading. A reader who was conversant with both serious fiction and various popular genres could decide during the process of reading *The Man with the Golden Arm* that the book had been mispackaged and that he or she should be reading it differently. Or, as I suspect is more often the case, a dedicated reader of pop fiction could decide that the novel was a failure because it did not deliver on the expectations created by its packaging. Furthermore, although any argument suggesting that texts are mutable and can be read in many ways based on aspects of material culture seems subversive regarding the idea of dependable, solid meaning, the roller-coaster ride of Algren's career suggests the more conservative idea that texts have firm features and resist certain sorts of readings or misreadings. The fact that Algren did not attain the popular fiction cult status that can eventually lead to canonical status—along the lines of that achieved by Dashiell

Hammett, Raymond Chandler, James M. Cain, or Jim Thompson—implies that pop fiction readers had trouble treating his texts as JD novels, junkie novels, or urban exposés despite the preinterpretive fields of particular editions.

Algren's canonical history is a complex and compelling one—one that gives us insight into key changes in American literary values since the 1930s. As the only novelist we have who combines the three most important aspects of twentieth-century American literature in a single package, Algren is unique in postwar American fiction. As the modernists he should be compared to—Hemingway, Ralph Ellison, Faulkner— Algren is a superb craftsman dedicated to his art: the depiction of the truth in language. As the naturalists, Algren believes literature should address the structures of oppression built into the class hierarchy of America by speaking for the most-marginalized members of our society. And as realists going back to Mark Twain, Algren believes literature can and should be written in the vernacular and that the writer must capture the humor and insight of the voice of the people. But in the great lurch rightward that American culture took during the 1950s and into the 1960s, any political content trumped everything else. All his artistry and craft—his ear for the language of the streets, the slang and energy of Chicago speech—was ignored or downgraded because Algren dared criticize America as "the one land where ownership and virtue are one."[22] Formalist critics dismissed him as a sentimentalist, a writer who was not just a bad serious writer, but one who was not a part of serious literary discourse, beneath the sophisticated reader's attention.

While the critics who dismissed Algren as subliterary helped ruin his career, Algren himself played into their characterization of him as less than serious by writing biting satiric attacks, wherein he gave his harshest critics comical nicknames. The appallingly inaccurate 1955 film adaptation of *The Man with the Golden Arm*, directed by Otto Preminger and starring Frank Sinatra, was the first mainstream Hollywood movie to depict drug addiction, and it too contributed to a general sense that Algren was a mere hack, a writer of junkie stories. Algren himself wrote that *The Man with the Golden Arm* was forgotten because of "a presentation which confused it, in the public mind, with a cheap biography of Frank Sinatra."[23]

Algren's contemporary return to serious status, another upward swoop of the roller coaster, is communicated to potential readers by the material form his novels are published in today. Starting with the Seven Stories Press reissues of *The Neon Wilderness* and *The Man with the Golden Arm* in 1989, Algren has been on the shelves of bookstores throughout the English-speaking world in trade paperbacks with covers usually featuring understated, stark black-and-white photos of Algren by Stephen Deutsch or Shay. The physical form of these editions—larger size, heavier paper, higher price—along with scholarly introductions and other apparatus identify Algren as a serious writer for readers unfamiliar with him, just as the early paperbacks marked him as a mere writer of pulp fiction. As we study Algren's works and his critical reception, we must keep in mind the complex dynamic of material culture and textual representation that simultaneously creates and reflects that reputation.

Notes

1. Barbara Herrnstein Smith, "Contingencies of Value," 5–39, in *Canons*, ed. Robert Von Hallberg (Chicago: University of Chicago Press, 1984), 15.
2. Thomas L. Bonn, *Heavy Traffic and High Culture: New American Library as Literary Gatekeeper in the Paperback Revolution* (New York: Meridian, 1990), 2.
3. Thomas L. Bonn, *Under Cover: An Illustrated History of American Mass-Market Paperbacks* (New York: Penguin, 1982), 21.
4. Jackie Merri Meyer, quoted in Julie Lasky, "Design for the Masses," 29–33, in *Design Culture: An Anthology of Writing from the AIGA Journal of Graphic Design*, ed. Steven Heller and Marie Finamore (New York: Allworth Press, 1997), 30.
5. E. D. Hirsch Jr., *Validity in Interpretation* (New Haven, Conn.: Yale University Press, 1967), 78–79.
6. Ibid., 86.
7. Stanley Fish, *Is There a Text in This Class? The Authority of Interpretive Communities* (Cambridge, Mass.: Harvard University Press, 1980), 322, 326.
8. Peter J. Rabinowitz, *Before Reading: Narrative Conventions and the Politics of Interpretation* (Columbus: Ohio State University Press, 1987), 26–27.
9. Mary Louise Pratt, *Toward a Speech Act Theory of Literary Discourse* (Bloomington: Indiana University Press, 1977), 120.
10. Rabinowitz, *Before Reading*, 186–87.
11. Leslie A. Fiedler, "The Noble Savages of Skid Row," *The Reporter*, January 12, 1956, 43–44.

12. James B. Twitchell, *Carnival Culture: The Trashing of Taste in America* (New York: Columbia University Press, 1992), 108.

13. Richard Ohmann, "The Shaping of a Canon: U.S. Fiction, 1960–75," in *Canons*, 377–401.

14. Bonn, *Under Cover*, 55, 56.

15. Ibid., 55.

16. See Lee Server's *Over My Dead Body: The Sensational Age of the American Paperback: 1945–1955* (San Francisco: Chronicle Books, 1994) and *Danger Is My Business: An Illustrated History of the Fabulous Pulp Magazines, 1896-1963* (San Francisco: Chronicle Books, 1993).

17. Bonn, *Under Cover*, 56.

18. Ibid., 56.

19. See Jane P. Tompkins, *Sensational Designs: The Cultural Work of American Fiction, 1790–1860* (New York: Oxford University Press, 1985).

20. Bonn, *Under Cover*, 91.

21. Ohmann, "The Shaping of a Canon," 388.

22. Nelson Algren, *The Man with the Golden Arm: 50th Anniversary Critical Edition*, ed. William J. Savage Jr. and Daniel Simon (New York: Seven Stories Press, 1999), 19.

23. Nelson Algren, *Chicago: City on the Make* (1951; repr., Chicago: University of Chicago Press, 1989), 94.

Hanging with Nelson Algren: A Brief Look at the Author and His Milieu

Warren Leming

We owe as much to Nelson Algren as the Dubliners do to James Joyce, the Berliners to Alfred Döblin and Bertolt Brecht, and the Parisians to Walter Benjamin and Marcel Proust. Algren is not noted as a historian of Chicago's past, but he was one. The city has long been the home of the class struggle, but in a world in which Margaret Thatcher can announce, "There is no such thing as Society" and George Bush can claim, "No classes," it has ceased to be a media-acceptable idea.

Come the Civil War, Chicago was among the fastest-growing cities in the world. A rail and shipping hub essential to the Union War effort, the city supplied the Western armies. Had you migrated to Chicago in 1865, you would have encountered a city of tremendous vitality, famed for its exploitation, its insatiable need for labor, its foreign populations, its brothels, its ward bosses, and a White Anglo-Saxon Protestant (WASP) merchant class of extraordinary pretension and power. Chicago was the site of a huge slaughtering and meat-processing facility known as the stockyards and a river so polluted by contamination from tanneries and leatherworks that it stank and frothed with offal.

Chicago by the 1880s had seen a huge German immigration, much of it skilled labor and much of it radical. German immigrants moved to Chicago to find work as carpenters, joiners, teamsters, bricklayers, barrel makers, tailors, and shoemakers, and they took their politics with them: not just Karl Marx but Johann Most, Mikhail Bakunin, Peter Kropotkin, Ferdinand Lasalle, and a thousand shades between. In the interests of long-term defamation, the local newspapers dubbed all of them anarchists and reported on their annual picnic, which drew forty-thousand people to commemorate the Paris Commune. Chicago's moneyed classes after 1871 were haunted by the memory of the commune and its worker uprising. The fortunes made during and after the Civil War were large, even by the standards of that mercantilist day: Armour and Swift in meatpacking, McCormick in farm tools and newspapers, Medill in publishing, Leiter and Field in real estate and retail merchandise, Palmer in land speculation and hotels, Pullman in railway cars. Fortunes in the hundreds of millions of dollars at a time were made when a workingman often made just over a dollar a day. Algren would point derisively to the Chicago Art Institute, whose board was composed of those identified with the city's old anti-Semite, antiforeigner mandarins and whose collection of French Impressionists (purchased by European agents) helped create the modern art market. Algren's point was that working people did not go to the museum because they knew what it had cost them in blood and sweat to send a rich man's agents to Europe to purchase the fruits of French culture while they were exploited at home.

In the 1850s there were riots when the city's civic leaders threatened to close the beer halls. The 1860s saw the Civil War and a quantum jump in business activity and exploitation. The 1870s saw labor agitation, a railroad strike, and occupation by federal troops during which thirty people were shot down and the rail yards burned. The 1880s saw more agitation for unions and the eight-hour workday, culminating in the Haymarket trial and hangings. The 1890s saw the Pullman strike, with more labor violence and police retaliation. By the turn of the century, even the merchant class wanted to see an end to violence, which had continued unabated for half a century. The astronomical Chicago fortunes pointed the way to one of the greatest labor incidents of the nineteenth century: the Haymarket trial, which resulted after a bomb was thrown at a public meeting in 1886 and eight men were indicted. The bomb thrower was never found. The men were tried for advocating an eight-hour day, and unionism. Four were executed, one was murdered in his cell, and three received life imprisonment. They were pardoned in 1894 by the then-governor John Altgeld, at the cost of his political career. The Chicago merchants destroyed him. Altgeld had said, "The day I pardon those men, my political career is finished."[1]

The eight-hour workday had been federal law since 1867, but it was simply ignored. Marshall Field's store sold on a cash-only basis and would extend no credit. Field did $50 million a year in business and paid no income tax. It was a world without social security, health benefits, unions, protected bargaining, or an eight-hour workday. These are benefits that corporations now claim they offer workers, failing to note that people died to secure these rights. These were the days before public relations mitigated the prose and refined the tactics of the rapacious and well-heeled Joseph Medill, who ran the *Tribune* and engineered vicious attacks on the Haymarket defendants. In 1890, Medill was asked to testify before Congress on labor agitation and working conditions in Chicago. Medill said, "The chief cause of the impecunious condition of the millions of the wage classes is their own improvidence and misdirected efforts. Too many are trying to live without labor . . . and many squander their earnings on intoxicating drinks, cigars, and amusements."[2] It is as perfect a piece of Calvinist self-justification as the nineteenth century would produce. Medill and the city's merchants backed the preacher and reformer Dwight L. Moody, whose sermons were said to prevent working people from agitating. It is still a successful technique in the United States, where promercantilist, procorporate right-wingers now dominate the conservative religious agendas through television. Where Mammon is God, God proclaims Mammon.

Algren is from that old Chicago Left culture, a culture whose defining moment occurred in the Haymarket riots and then the Pullman strike, which followed in 1894. George Mortimer Pullman, a multimillionaire, had created a model city for his workers. He had their rents and other necessities deducted directly from their paychecks and required that they attend the company church. When he died within a few years of the strike, his family buried him at Graceland Cemetery under tons of steel and concrete for fear his former employees would despoil the body. The railroads had made the meat packers rich, and by 1913, seven years after Upton Sinclair wrote *The Jungle* (1906), a book about conditions in the Chicago meatpacking houses, a Senate investigation produced the first pure food and drug laws. Sinclair had sought to change working conditions in the packing and slaughtering plants. He was later to remark bitterly, "I aimed for their hearts and wound up hitting them in the stomach."[3]

In 1913 John D. Rockefeller was the most-hated man in America. His gun thugs aided by the national guard had shot down thirty-five men, women, and children in Colorado during a miner's strike. Rockefeller's response was to hire Ivy Lee, who with Edward Bernays was to found modern public relations. At Lee's urging, Rockefeller created the Rockefeller Foundation, which continued his financial support of the University of Chicago. Newspapers were paid to photograph the millionaire giving dimes to small children while extolling the virtues of unfettered capitalism. Within thirty years, Rockefeller and his sons had been rehabilitated: they were now fit for public office and acclamation, and a whole new class of exploiters had hard evidence of the fantastic spin benefits of public relations. Lee had won and in rehabilitating Rockefeller helped extend marketing, advertising, and public relations: the image industries, which now dominate contemporary life.

Algren disliked the corporate type—whether academic or industrial. He detested Saul Bellow, the University of Chicago fixture who won the 1976 Nobel Prize in Literature. The feeling was mutual. He shared a practiced disdain for the University of Chicago, calling it a company town. One of our discussions prompted this song, which I reworked for a satirical review years later:

> If you like English lit. They know just whom to cite
> It's publish or it's perish; it's where they teach it right.
> And if you like Economics there are Nobel prizewinners
> Ketchup is a vegetable when Dr. Friedman makes your dinner
> And if you want to write a thesis, there's sociology
> Researching just off campus, in the midst of incredible poverty
> You won't want just one degree, after you've bitten the apple
> And if you're into sinning, there's Rockefeller Chapel.
> Yes where logic is the purest, who needs the senior prom?
> Why they even gave up football, just to build the bomb.
>
> On Chicago's old South Side, there's a University
> Rockefeller built it with what's called usury
> A little bit of Gothic splendor in the midst of misery
> All hail the Marooned,
> The good old U. of C.[4]

Algren had studied the state-financed campaigns of intimidation, which have defined America's class struggle for well over a century: the Red Scare of 1919 with its deportations, the Klan-state alliances in the American South and Midwest, the corporate antilabor policies of the 1930s, and J. Edgar Hoover and Joseph McCarthy's attack on progressives in the 1940s and 1950s. Chicago's Red Squad, now forced out of existence, was long a fact of local law enforcement. Algren termed the law a form of entrapment and once planned a novel on the theme. He headed a committee seeking justice for the Rosenbergs and consequently had his passport pulled. He had seen Abraham Lincoln Brigade veterans such as Eddie Balchowsky, Sid Harris, and Johnny Rossen harassed for decades by the Federal Bureau of Investigation. Their crime: premature antifascism, that Orwellian phrase with which the House Un-American Activities Committee and Hoover justified wiretaps, prison, and intimidation.

With the postwar period, the once vibrant Left culture, which Algren had emerged from, was suddenly the stuff of nostalgia, consigned to the media-driven memory hole. Should you go to Chicago today there is a small plaque commemorating the Haymarket incident and written in the generalist language necessary to careful obscurity. It is near a pedestal, which once supported a statue, honoring the police. Twice blown up in the sixties, the statue has since been returned to the safety of the local police academy.

Algren's *Chicago: City on the Make* (1951) is a lyrical history of the town laced with Algren's bitterness and too close to the truth to be acceptable to the chamber of commerce. My play *Cold Chicago: A Haymarket Fable* (2001) was inspired by *Chicago*, as was "The Song of the Great Prairie":

Once all of this was Prairie
As far as the eye could see
And then one day the traders came
Bringing guns and whiskey
Bringing guns and whiskey
And singing loudly: Amen
Singing: Goddammit Amen.

The traders came up river
Cursing the day they were born

Trading whiskey for furs
And living on Indian corn
Oh, Living on Indian corn.

Guns and whiskey by day
By night they prayed alone
They were in debt to Astor,
We must reap what we have sown
Oh, Reap what we have sown.

Man was born to sin
Man was born to repent.
But only guns and whiskey
Pay back what has been lent
Oh, pay back what has been lent.

Once all of this was Prairie
As far as the eye could see
And then one day the traders came
Bringing guns and whiskey
Bringing guns and whiskey
And singing loudly: Amen
Singing: Goddammit Amen.[5]

Algren for a time had a local celebrity. Briefly, he had a street named after him, but the residents in the area, confused about and hostile toward a man they believed had offended the Polish people, voted that the signs be removed and the street renamed. Today there is a street sign under the "real" street sign, designating Algren Avenue, which is the work of the Algren Committee. Is there a point when his legend overcomes Algren? A point when the two meld just this side of a major B movie? Algren's caustic legacy may just be at that point. Algren gains to a belated fame, long after its benefits were denied him. Algren's sad affair with Simone de Beauvoir has been well publicized and has had not a little to do with his rehabilitation—an irony he might have appreciated. Chicago and Algren are of a piece. He knew Leon Despres well, in the days when he was the only alderman in the city council not hostage to Mayor Daley's absolute dictatorship. Algren spent his best years in Chicago—and I think he tried to get at something that no one has since achieved. *Chicago* will still give you more of the town than the town wants known. Chicago's vastness, its loneliness, and the life of the place are difficult to get at: Chicago is a place like the truth, which resists comprehension.

Algren lived in Wicker Park, once the old German anarchist community. Even the German beer barons were forbidden the expensive downtown areas by the WASP aristocracy, the Palmers, the Fields, the McCormicks, the Medills, and the Pullmans, who were loath to have the Germans, Jews, Bohemians, and Poles next door. So the "foreigners," as they were dubbed, settled in Wicker Park. The area was linked to the Loop, the downtown area by Milwaukee Avenue, known as Lunch Pail Avenue. The workingmen heading downtown carried their lunch pails as they walked: streetcars were too expensive. Wicker Park's foreigners were forbidden to sing when they buried the Haymarket martyrs; instead, they threw roses as the funeral cortege passed on its way out to Waldheim, the old German cemetery in Forest Park. The statue erected there to the Haymarket dead was recently designated—a hundred years late—a national historic site worthy of preservation, unlike the memory of the martyrs themselves, long since carefully forgotten in the town where they were lynched.

Algren proposed a monument to the Haymarket defendants. Dedicated to Albert Parsons, the monument was to contain Louis Lingg's challenge: "I despise your order, your laws, your force propped authority. Hang me for it."[6] It is a monument that will never be built. It is axiomatic, even today, that the words *labor* and *class* are sure ways not to be funded by the city fathers and the local agencies. This came home to me when we attempted to stage a labor history festival in Wicker Park and were refused permission, by the city, to use a public park. That was in 1998: just 112 short years since the Haymarket riots. The local media are best summed-up by the *Chicago Tribune*. It began under Medill, who had discovered and promoted Lincoln for the presidency and then made the *Chicago Tribune* the voice of the moneyed. You can still see some of the public bathhouses he had built to cleanse the poor—and Northwestern University has its Medill School of Journalism. It has all been done very neatly, even to the Chicago Historical Society's brochure on the Haymarket bomb throwing and trial, written conveniently by a *Chicago Tribune* employee.

I met Algren many years ago in the bar of a theater called the Second City. The site was later sold by the city to a real estate developer for pennies, though it fronts on Lincoln Park and was worth several millions. The developer was later forced to repurchase the land for something approximating its actual value. A local columnist had gotten wind of the deal and blown the whistle. Even in Chicago, the truth will sometimes out. Algren, when I met him, lived in a no-man's-land between his previous success and the slow descent into a semianonymous state that Chicago reserves for those who have written well about the place. James T. Farrell was long since gone, another victim to the memory hole, and with him the memory of Theodore Dreiser, Sherwood Anderson, and the rest of the "realists" whose stock had fallen, propelled by American academics' postmodernist confusions. Near Tooker Place, just off Dearborn Street, was the site of the Dill Pickle Club, where the literati had gathered in decades past. Slim Brundage, once the bouncer at the Dill Pickle, opened a place on State Street in the 1950s called the College of Complexes, which still served to draw together the Wobblies, anarchists, Lefties, and locals. The McCarthy period and a well-financed provincialism—always a benchmark of the town—had put an end to the more-vocal radicals.

The fringes of Chicago were to resurface twice in the 1960s: once, with the Beats, and again, in 1968, when the antiwar movement was copper fitted to attempts at hippie community. Algren had no time for either. Algren, I think, resented the attention given Jack Kerouac and Gregory Corso and Allen Ginsberg and the rest. The Beats mix of hyperbolic mysticism, soft pharmaceuticals, and Whitmanesque rhapsodizing were not his tastes. Algren, when I last saw him in the late 1970s, had had enough of Chicago. He had gone east. We corresponded over a plan to dramatize his short stories for the local public television station: our collective fate in the hands of a man who had once produced Dick Clark's *American Bandstand*—a teenage dance show—and then had the foresight to move from teen schlock to the high-art pretensions of public television. Our project was shot down, and the station maintains, to the present moment, its tradition of producing little beyond the mandatory while proclaiming itself an alternative to the vast wasteland of American media. The independent, freethinking intellectual of Algren's type, by the late sixties, had almost completely disappeared. Corporations and universities preferred another kind of intellectual, and they got them; have them yet. Infrequently, Algren might appear at O'Rourke's on North Avenue, a bar where the corporate journalists hung out. Algren was not really a journalist, and there seemed a time barrier between Algren, who had emerged from the Depression years and then the war, and the corporate writers who had come along in the 1950s and 1960s.

Wicker Park, Algren's old neighborhood, had changed. Latinos in the 1950s had replaced the Poles and Ukrainians and East Europeans of whom Algren had written. White flight introduced blockbusting real estate developers and the redlining banks that would not lend to the poor. Loners have a low survival rate, and Algren did not belong to anybody's party. I remember seeing him debate with some Black Panthers in the 1960s, and the confusion was complete on both sides. This was about the time that the state's attorney in Chicago had shot an apartment to pieces and in the process killed Fred Hampton and Mark Clark, effectively decapitating the Black Panther movement in Chicago. The city later settled with the relatives for a million or two after decades of wrangling in the courts. The wheels of justice grind exceedingly slow in Chicago, and by the time they stop you may no longer be vertical or eligible for compensation. Chicago in the 1930s, with its upfront color lines and tradition of police brutality running all the way back to Haymarket, had been a hard school for Algren. He was not optimistic about student-led movements or attempts at social justice by people he considered naive and woolly-headed. West Madison Street, with its flophouses and gin hells, has been torn down and replaced with city-financed public housing—the deal engineered by a real estate developer who made himself a millionaire in the process.

Algren's apartment was a third-floor walk-up. Its cluttered interior featured a lady who would cook using his limited supply of crockery. A Victorian redbrick, it is still there, adorned with a plaque to his memory—put up by the Algren Committee. The plaque was quickly followed by a *Chicago Tribune* historical marker that manages to reduce Algren's bitter history to something as bland and generic as a used-car ad. Algren had grown up on the South Side, where the topics on offer tend to be baseball and work. Ever a Sox fan, he liked Comiskey Park, the cavernous temple to the gods of the bat in Bridgeport, home of the Daley family and the mayor who ruled Chicago for most of Algren's life. There was still a strip along Division Street where Phyllis' Musical Inn and the Czar Bar went to 2 a.m. and Leo's Lunchroom opened at 7 a.m. with a hangover breakfast of eggs and bacon, coffee and toast. But Division Street, as had Algren, had changed. There had been a group that knew him, now long gone: Eddie Balchowsky, the one-armed piano player veteran of the Spanish Civil War who often gave away his paintings and drawings, Sid Harris, the union photographer. Sid had been with Eddie in the Lincoln Brigade, and the story was that Eddie had played piano for Paul Robeson in Madrid: Robeson singing songs in eight languages for the men of the Loyalist brigades. Eddie had retuned from the Civil War in Spain addicted to morphine, the result of a wound that cost him his arm.

Chicago to this day has its Daley family well entrenched. The mayor and something like a hundred of his relatives all have well-paying city jobs. They are the Irish who manage the place after years fighting to get in on the game. Chicago's political bosses found what had been discovered elsewhere in America: the old class enemy was ultimately an ally. The well-heeled, whether real estate developer or society type, today help fund Chicago politics. The key to all of this lies in real estate speculation and city contracts. Chicago remains one of the great lockstep political operations. A local progressive alderman who has voted with the Daley machine 85 percent of the time was recently almost unseated by the mayor's forces. She just was not cooperating. This Stalinist approach has paid huge dividends for the well-placed people who pass building codes and zoning laws: Chicago's politicians.

The last time I saw Algren he was headed out of town, to the East Coast. There had been a final fire sale at the old apartment, and almost everything sold, from the typewriter to the cracked crockery. I keep going back to Chicago, in the twenty-odd years since Algren died. And I still carry some of his vision of the place with me. The town's never been the same since Algren described it—tribute enough to someone who said that if you get just one block right, it's enough for one lifetime. And the good citizens, whether they like it or not, are still indebted to him. Algren once quoted Eugene V. Debs, Socialist candidate for president just after

World War I, who had said, "[W]hile there is a soul in prison, I am not free."[7] Algren stands with Debs and that radical America—long since carefully, quietly, and meticulously forgotten.

Notes

1. Quoted in *Haymarket Scrapbook*, ed. Dave Roediger and Franklin Rosemont (Chicago: Charles H. Kerr, 1986), 172.

2. See Report of the [Education and Labor] Committee of the Senate upon the Relations between Capital and Labor, and Testimony taken by the Committee, 4 vols (Washington, D.C., 1885), 2, 959.

3. See *Encyclopedia of the American Left*, ed. Mari Jo Buhle, Paul Buhle, and Dan Georgakas (Urbana: University of Illinois Press, 1992), 701.

4. "The U. of C. Fight Song," in *Weimer*, a show directed by Warren Leming and performed at Cross Currents Cabaret, Chicago, 1984.

5. Warren Leming, *Cold Chicago: A Haymarket Fable* (Chicago: Charles H. Kerr, 2001), 108.

6. See Louis Lingg, "Address to the Court, Famous Speeches of the Chicago Anarchists" (Chicago 1912) in *Haymarket Scrapbook*, 47.

7. Eugene V. Debs, quoted in Nick Salvatore, *Eugene V. Debs: Citizen and Socialist* (Urbana: University of Illinois Press, 1982), 295.

The Nelson Algren Archive at the Ohio State University Libraries

Elva Griffith

On April 2, 1965, Nelson Algren wrote the following letter addressed to the Offices of the President, Ohio State University:

> Dear Sir,
>
> I am informed that interest in mss of mine has been expressed at Ohio State.
>
> I would appreciate being advised to whom I should address myself in order to identify this interest.
>
> Specifically, it is the letters of Mme. Simone de Beauvoir whose purchase I am interested in arranging.
>
> Cordially,
>
> Nelson Algren

Algren had recently received his manuscripts back from Lewis Feldman, a dealer in New York who had told Algren he had a buyer for all of his manuscripts. After having them for about a year, Feldman told him there were problems: give him more time and he could find a buyer. But Algren had decided it was time to act as his own agent and demanded everything back. Simone de Beauvoir's letters had not been sent to New York and were not part of his deal with Feldman. Besides Ohio State, he had offered the letters to Texas and to Gallimard, de Beauvoir's publisher.

Algren was trying to get enough money from the sale of the material to keep him while he was working on a new novel. He contacted Ohio State because four years earlier, in 1961, we had acquired directly from him four manuscript drafts of *The Man with the Golden Arm* (1949). Also, he must certainly have known that Feldman had made an offer to us of twenty-five thousand dollars for his archive. Algren was to get twenty thousand dollars.

Richard Ploch was curator of Rare Books at that time and had seen the manuscripts in Feldman's New York shop in December. Despite Ploch's urging, no move was made to accept Feldman's offer. I think Algren's letter was just the push Ohio State needed to reconsider.[1]

In May, Rex Beckham, assistant director of the libraries, visited Algren in Chicago and suggested "he consider working out an arrangement with a single institution where all his materials would be housed and where their research value would be greatly enhanced by their magnitude and totality." Algren agreed he should —and would like to—do that. He told Beckham that he intended to keep everything in the future—anything he writes and letters he receives, but not laundry lists. James T. Farrell, Algren told Beckham, "began to write and save for posterity years ago. He even saves laundry slips."

In Beckham's report of their conversation, he wrote that Algren would be in favor of a long-term purchase—as a steady income for four or five years and as a way to beat the Bureau of Internal Revenue. "He asked if we did not have a university hall which we could sell—or even a president." He also told Beckham that de Beauvoir is a very minor writer, a reporter with little imagination and no color or humor.[2]

In June, Beckham telephoned Algren in Saint Louis. Beckham asked him how an offer of fifteen hundred to seventeen hundred dollars sounded to him for de Beauvoir's letters. Algren said it sounded low, though he did not know what they were worth. He said he had hoped for four or five times that.[3]

In July, Matthew J. Bruccoli, a professor in the English Department at Ohio State, phoned Beckham from Algren's apartment in Chicago to inform him that Algren was willing to sell his manuscripts for twenty thousand dollars to be paid in three annual installments. The collection being offered included all the material Feldman had offered Ohio State the previous December. It did not include any additional material, but Algren told Bruccoli that he would hold for Ohio State any other manuscripts he now had and any he would produce in the future. We would have the right of first refusal on these, the first offer to be made in three years. Beckham's memo to Lewis Branscomb, director of the libraries, concluded, "Matt [Bruc-coli] had two words of advice: Grab it!"[4] And we did. The agreement was finalized in Chicago in July 1965. Twenty years later, by the way, Bruccoli published his *Nelson Algren: A Descriptive Bibliography.*

That 1965 purchase included material for all of Algren's works up to *Notes from a Sea Diary: Hemingway All the Way* (1965). There are various drafts—some of them extensively revised—and many fragments of drafts of *Somebody in Boots* (1935), *Never Come Morning* (1942), *The Neon Wilderness* (1947), *The Man with the Golden Arm, Chicago: City on the Make* (1951), *A Walk on the Wild Side* (1956), and *Who Lost an American?* (1963). There are also typesetting copies and galley proofs for most of those. A few examples of the material we acquired at that time are Algren's notes in two pocket-size notebooks that were used as source material for *Somebody in Boots* and later for *A Walk on the Wild Side*; a set of rules for jailhouse conduct made up by the inmates, which Algren took with him when he was released from the county jail of Alpine, Texas, in February 1934; extensive notes on dialect, idioms, and characters as well as notes from police line-ups that Algren attended to gather source material used in *The Man with the Golden Arm*; adding what we had just acquired to the four manuscript drafts that were purchased in 1961, over twenty-five hundred pages of manuscript material for *The Man with the Golden Arm*; and the earliest draft of *A Walk on the Wild Side,* which is a copy of *Somebody in Boots* with revisions made directly in the book: Algren had written on nearly every page and all end papers.

We did not get Algren's letters from de Beauvoir. I personally find it interesting that Algren was willing to sell the drafts, the notes, and all of his manuscripts from *Somebody in Boots* to *Who Lost an American?* for twenty thousand dollars and was hoping for at least six thousand dollars—even as much as eighty-five hundred dollars—for those letters alone. For whatever reason, he did not sell de Beauvoir's letters. Ohio State acquired them from Algren's estate after Algren's death.

Nelson Algren died in May 1981. Under the curatorship of Robert Tibbetts in 1982, the libraries purchased from Algren's estate the archival material and library on hand at the time of his death. Ohio State now had a nearly comprehensive archive for the study of Algren's work and life. The acquisition added literary manuscripts, correspondence, books from his personal library, and interesting Algren memorabilia.

Letters from de Beauvoir constitute a major component of the correspondence, written from 1947 to 1964 and covering the period from their first meeting through to the breakup of their relationship. They are handwritten in English. As love letters they are charming, but they are more than that. They are filled with extensive literary discussion of de Beauvoir's own and Algren's work and that of other writers, both French and American. The letters have now been published, originally in French translation by Gallimard in 1997 and in 1998 by The New Press under the title *A Transatlantic Love Affair: Letters to Nelson Algren.*

We also have the journal kept by both de Beauvoir and Algren of their trip from Chicago to Mexico to New York in 1948. It has sixty-seven pages with her daily entry at the top and Algren's below, usually taking up the majority of the page.

We acquired letters written to Algren by many other writers, including letters from James T. Farrell, Ernest Hemingway, and Richard Wright. Besides correspondence, the 1982 purchase was rich in literary manuscripts. We now had typescripts of various drafts and portions of drafts for *Notes from a Sea Diary*, *The Last Carousel* (1973), and *The Devil's Stocking* (1983), as well as for most of his short stories and poems, many of them with extensive holograph revision. Most of Algren's manuscripts are typed with various amounts of holograph revision, meaning that the revisions were handwritten by Algren. Many pages have typing and/or writing on their versos that has nothing in common with what is on their front except Algren.

With this collection were multiple drafts of *The Devil's Stocking*, a novel based on the career of Rubin "Hurricane" Carter. Algren spent the last years of his life researching and writing about Carter, a top contender for the middleweight boxing championship, who was convicted of triple murder in a highly controversial trial of the late 1960s. It was Algren's last novel and was published posthumously, first in German, titled *Calhoun* (1981), and then in English under the title *The Devil's Stocking*. Among these drafts are manuscripts of Algren's first nonfiction version of the Carter case and of "Chinatown," the first fiction version of the story.

There are drafts for "The Yellow and the White," "The Yellow and the Wan," "The Man in the Hotel Mirror," "The Yellow and the Black," and "Nothing Happens in the Heart." There are about 350 pages, mostly typescript with extensive holograph revisions and with drafts of other pieces on the versos of many of them. At the time the appraisal was done for this collection, these pages were in an envelope labeled by Algren "Love in an Iron Rain/Unpublished Material."

There are typescripts for "Traces of H" and for "Barefoot with Shoes On" or "The Real Thing" or "No Shoes for Novak." "Traces of H" is on the versos of a portion of a draft of a filmscript of *The Man with the Golden Arm*. There are typescripts of many different poems and drafts of poems. Titles include "Tricks out of Time Long Gone," "I Heard the Monkey Scratching," "Lightless Arena," "Moon of the Arfy-Darfy," and "Ode to an Absconding Bookie." We have the original copy of "So Help Me," Algren's first published story, which appeared in the August 1933 issue of the periodical called *Story*. And we are very proud to have the Saturday, March 6, 1920, issue of "The Chicago Evening News," the only copy of this Chicago newspaper, which was published, edited, written, and composed by Nelson Algren at age eleven.

The purchase from Algren's estate added memorabilia valuable for the study of his life. Algren liked to make collages. We have his collages of de Beauvoir, of portraits of his family, of Southeast Asia and the Vietnam War, of horse racing, and of baseball. We also have many photographs of boxers.

We have his scrapbooks, dating from the 1930s on, which are filled with magazine printings of his stories, reviews of his works, and various clippings regarding Algren, some with annotations by him. There is a large collection of photographs, many of them by Algren taken on travels to North Africa, Vietnam, and elsewhere in Asia, as well as a large number in Mexico. These include photographs of de Beauvoir.

Algren's personal library totaled over twelve hundred volumes. There are first and early editions of his books, including many foreign editions. Among his books are presentation copies from such writers as Hemingway, Joseph Heller, Wright, de Beauvoir, Jean-Paul Sartre, and Carl Sandburg, many of them with marginalia by Algren and his distinctive cat signature. Among the books in his general library are fiction, art books, books by and about Russian writers, books on boxing, books on baseball, books on Chicago, and books on Vietnam. The collection is immense, and I regret to say it is still not thoroughly organized. We are working now on getting detailed descriptions of our collections on the Web, so Internet users will soon be able to browse our finding aid for Algren online.

There is also much Algren material that has been added since the purchase from his estate. Although complete descriptions of these holdings are not going to be available anytime soon, short records will appear to alert researchers that we have this material. I want to mention briefly those various collections, because they do much to strengthen and enrich the Algren archive.

In 1986 we obtained material from Carl Weissner, German translator of *Calhoun*.

In 1992 the libraries purchased two very fine collections of letters under the curatorship of Geoffrey Smith, who had just that year become Head of Rare Books. Amanda Algren had decided to sell her collection of letters and photographs that she had received from Nelson during their two marriages. There are about seventy letters and postcards written from the mid-1940s through the 1950s. These are really wonderful letters. Algren talks about everything from a black kitten that just found itself a home to his anguish over the painful struggle to free himself from the marriage to Amanda.

Also in 1992 Roger Groening, as did Amanda, thought it was time to find a safe harbor for his Algren material. Groening had received about two hundred pages of letters from Algren covering a fifteen-year span beginning in the mid-1960s.

In 1993 the libraries very wisely purchased the archive of Bettina Drew, compiled for her biography *Nelson Algren: A Life on the Wild Side*. Drew's archive contains notes, original manuscript material, many letters to her about Algren, photographs taken by Art Shay and Stephen Deutsch, snapshots of Algren as a child with his family in Chicago, contact prints of Guatemala and Mexico taken by Algren and de Beauvoir during their 1948 trip, and extensive photocopied collections of Algren's letters, many uncollected elsewhere; transcripts and tapes of interviews; and an extensive clipping file containing most of Algren's uncollected magazine appearances. Just last summer we added to the Bettina Drew/Algren Archive Drew's collected materials related to *The Texas Stories of Nelson Algren* (1995).

Also last year we purchased a collection of thirty-four letters and postcards Algren wrote to Jack Conroy, dating from 1933 to 1958.

Back in 1965, the purchase of the Algren collection was considered a bold step forward in our rare book acquisitions and a gamble. I think it is safe to say that Ohio State University would not have his collection today if Algren had not written that letter on April 2. One thing is sure: by betting on Algren, we did not lose.

Notes

All references are taken from Ohio State University, Rare Books and Manuscripts.

1. Richard A. Ploch to H. A. Kritzer, January 6, 1965.
2. Rex Beckham to Dr. Lewis Branscomb, et al., May 25, 1965: Report of a conversation with Nelson Algren on May 24, 1965.
3. Rex Beckham to Dr. Lewis Branscomb, et al.: Report of a phone conversation with Nelson Algren on June 14, 1965.
4. Rex Beckham to Dr. Lewis Branscomb, July 8, 1965.

Contributors

KASIA BODDY teaches in the Department of English at University College London. She has published articles on a variety of American authors and topics. Her book on the cultural representation of boxing, *Great Hopes*, is in its final stages.

BETTINA DREW's first book, *Nelson Algren: A Life on the Wild Side*, was a finalist for the *Chicago Sun-Times* Book of the Year in 1989 and received a Special Citation from PEN and a Fellowship in Non-Fiction Literature from the New York Foundation for the Arts. Her second book, *Crossing the Expendable Landscape*, received a Special Citation in the PEN New England Award. Her essays and book reviews have appeared in the *Yale Review*, *The Chicago Tribune*, *The Washington Post*, *Threepenny Review*, *Virginia Quarterly Review*, *The Nation*, and many other magazines. She is writing a biography of Andrew Jackson (forthcoming) and is assistant professor of English and Creative Writing at the University of Missouri, Columbia.

CAROLINE GOTTSCHALK-DRUSCHKE is currently pursuing a doctoral degree at Northwestern University in Evanston, Illinois. She has previously presented a paper on Nelson Algren at the 3 Cities Conference in Nottingham, United Kingdom, in April 2003, and at the Annual M/MLA Conference in Chicago in November 2003. Her research and writing center on urban literature of post–World War II America and Britain, with a particular emphasis on canon formation, the politics of exclusion, and representations of the city.

FRÉDÉRIC DUMAS was born in 1960. He is an assistant professor at Stendhal University-Grenoble, France. He is the author of *La quête identitaire et son inscription dans l'oeuvre de Nelson Algren* (The

Search for identity and its inscription in the work of Nelson Algren) (2001), from his doctoral thesis—the only one to date devoted to Nelson Algren in France. He has written several articles on Nelson Algren in French scholarly publications and regularly takes part in international symposiums on contemporary American literature in Europe and in the United States. His most recent published work is an article on Paul Auster's *New York Trilogy* in Villes de pierres, de toile, & de papier (2005).

JAMES R. GILES is presidential teaching professor of English at Northern Illinois University. He is the author of eight books, including *Violence in the Contemporary American Novel* (2000), *Understanding Hubert Selby, Jr.* (1998), *The Naturalistic Inner-City Novel in America* (1995), and *Confronting the Horror: The Novels of Nelson Algren* (1989). He is the coeditor of seven others: *Approaches to Teaching the Works of Louise Erdrich* (2004), *The James Jones Reader* (1991), and five volumes of the *Dictionary of Literary Biography on American Novelists Since World War II.*

ELVA GRIFFITH began working in The Ohio State University Libraries in 1969. Since 1992 she has been a library associate in its Rare Books & Manuscripts Library and is curator of its Irish collection.

STEPHEN HARDMAN has completed a Ph.D. dissertation entitled "Common People: Working Class Politics and Culture in the British and American Novel of the 1950s" at the University of Canterbury, New Zealand. His research interests include twentieth century working class literature and politics in Britain and the United States as well as contemporary political fiction.

WARREN LEMING is a writer/artist who divides his time between Chicago and Berlin. He is the author of *Cold Chicago: A Haymarket Fable* (2001), a play and essays based on the Haymarket affair. His Web site, coldchicagocompany.org, includes a comprehensive list of his work in video, film, music, the theater, and cultural criticism. He has written for *The Socialist*, *Lies of Our Times*, *The Heartland Journal*, *Context*, *Sklaven*, *Race Traitor*, and *Chicago Ink*. He was the founder of the Wilderness Road Band and has recorded for Columbia and Warner/Reprise Records. He currently directs the Cold Chicago Company theater in Chicago and is editing a series of essays on culture and politics.

PHILIP MCGOWAN is Senior Lecturer at Queen's University Belfast. His publications include the books *American Carnival: Seeing and Reading American Culture* (2001) and *Anne Sexton and Middle Generation Poetry: The Geography of Grief* (2004).

IAN PEDDIE is assistant professor of English at West Texas A&M University. He has taught classes on popular music and social protest, cultural studies, and modern British and American literature. His publications include essays on Langston Hughes, Nelson Algren, Thomas McGrath, radical literature, and popular music. He is the editor of *The Resisting Muse: Popular Music and Social Protest* (2006), and is currently working on a book about the Scottish author Irvine Welsh.

BILL SAVAGE was born, raised, and educated in Chicago, and that explains a lot of things. He wrote his doctoral dissertation on material aspects of literary culture and Nelson Algren's canonical status at Northwestern University, where he is an administrator and senior lecturer in the English Department. He coedited the *The Man with the Golden Arm: 50th Anniversary Critical Edition* (with Daniel Simon) and *Chicago: City on the Make: 50th Anniversary Edition, Newly Annotated* (with David Schmittgens).

ROBERT WARD lectures in American literature at St Martin's College, Lancaster. His doctoral dissertation was on motifs of imprisonment in the work of Nelson Algren, and he continues to give papers, and publish articles, on Algren, Left writing of the 1930s, and American prison writing. He is currently working on ideas of memoir in the recent work of Joan Didion.

Index